THE STORY OF
A HUMBLE CHRISTIAN

THE STORY OF
A HUMBLE CHRISTIAN

Ignazio Silone

Translated from the Italian by
William Weaver

1817

HARPER & ROW, PUBLISHERS

NEW YORK · EVANSTON · SAN FRANCISCO · LONDON

FIRST U.S. EDITION

STANDARD BOOK NUMBER: 06-013873-4

LIBRARY OF CONGRESS CATALOG CARD NUMBER: 79-95982

TRANSLATOR'S NOTE

As the reader will see, I have been inconsistent in translating names of people and places. Following common usage, I have rendered names of historical figures for the most part into English (e.g. Saint Benedict, Pope Boniface, Philip the Fair). Other names I have left in Italian. Similarly, I have translated the Abbey of the Holy Spirit, but not, for example, Santa Maria di Collemaggio.

This inconsistency is deliberate, but, I believe, justified.

W. W.

CONTENTS

Notes

WHAT REMAINS

The Beginning of a Search

In the provinces a secret is short-lived. At the foot of the steps of the provincial library today I met a literary friend, who immediately asked me, with a laugh: "You're not going to take up historical novels, are you?"

"I couldn't," I answered, thinking to cut the discussion short. "You know that as a writer I'm interested only in the present."

"True," he said, "but didn't you write somewhere that certain present situations have remote roots?"

My pretence didn't last long. The friend already knew of my visit yesterday to the city archives, where I had examined certain documents connected with Celestine V. In fact, this news has apparently aroused some odd comments in the little circle of my local acquaintances. My friend wanted to boast of how he had defended me by quoting from memory an essay of mine on fiction and the Southern "subsoil", in which I discussed Carlo Cafiero and the Italian anarchists of today, tracing their origins back to Joachim of Fiore.

"You're right," I said, finally confirming his suspicions. "I'm doing a bit of archaeology."

"Can you explain," my friend insisted, "why such a fascinating subject has never been dealt with by Italian writers? Of course, Dante referred to it; Petrarch discussed it in a forceful passage; but then afterwards? Nothing in Alfieri, nothing in Manzoni . . ."

"The ethical-religious problem became taboo," I said. "First we had the Renaissance, and then the Council of Trent."

"A purely Italian taboo," my friend said. "Georges Sand's *Spiridion* was inspired by the story of Joachim of Fiore. And even Lessing was interested in the Calabrian abbot."

We were walking towards the basilica of Santa Maria di Collemaggio, where that morning there was to be the usual annual commemoration of Celestine V's coronation, and as we walked along, we continued chatting. I mentioned some of my preliminary doubts: novel, essay, play? In any case, I am bent on reducing to a minimum the historical scenography. I am interested only in the conflicts of morals and thought.

"If I understand you correctly," my friend said, "it'll be a new version of *And He Did Hide Himself*, only set in the 14th century this time."

"Why not?" I answered. "In that play I introduced a Fra Joachim, and not entirely by chance."

What I meant was that between the new work and the preceding ones there will be no leap or rupture. Frankly I'm surprised when other writers boast of how different some new book of theirs is from their previous work; personally I like a coherence of content. If a writer puts all of himself in his writing (and what else can he put into it?) his work inevitably forms a single book. I've already said elsewhere that, if it had been in my power to change the commercial rules of literary society, I would have liked to spend my life writing and rewriting the same story, in the hope of understanding it at least, and of making it understood by others. In the Middle Ages there were monks who spent their lives painting the Holy Face, always the same face, though in reality the paintings were never quite identical. Now it's clear that I'm interested in the fate of a certain type of man, how a certain type of Christian fits into the machinery of the world, and I wouldn't know how to write about anything else.

"The Vatican Council," my friend said, "has revived some old issues that the hierarchy had shelved for hundreds of years, some of them dating as far back as the 14th century, when, thanks chiefly to Saint Francis, they had become a matter of public domain. But the Italian Church, on the whole, is now in the rearguard."

"There is a history of popular Italian Christianity," I observed, "which is distinct from the history of the hierarchy.

Since it isn't always written down in books, even cultivated laymen are unaware of it. This is why so many people wonder where Pope John sprang from, with his special inspiration and his style."

"Yes, he was a real surprise. Let's hope more follow."

The air filled with a mounting, disordered ringing of bells. On the broad street that leads to the basilica there was a dense flow of motor-cars and of poor people, which the police tried to arrange according to a plan of their own. Here and there we could hear a voice shouting: "You don't realize who I am." The shouts added vivacity to the crowd of little carts of the ice-cream vendors and the pedlars selling coloured balloons. "Is there a match being played today?" a distinguished-looking stranger asked me. "Do they play football on Sunday mornings in this city?"

"Satisfy my curiosity on one point," my friend asked after a little while. "In these visits of yours to convent libraries, I imagine you are obliged to meet some of the monks. Aren't you repelled by that?"

I didn't understand the question. My friend explained further: "Perhaps the right word is embarrassment or uneasiness," he said. "Are you able to be casual with monks?"

"I don't understand what you mean," I repeated. "Don't you consider them the same as other human beings?"

"Don't you feel an instinctive sense of repulsion when you're with them?" he insisted. "Don't they arouse the moral equivalent of the smell of incense?"

"Does something of that sort happen to you?" I asked, curious.

"Frankly, yes," he answered. "I don't believe it's an entirely personal reaction. I think every writer with a liberal or radical training . . ."

At that I understood what he meant. I interrupted him.

"Although you and I are about the same age," I said, "I come from a different background. I consider myself post-Risorgimento and perhaps even post-Marxist. Both in ideology and in sensibility."

At the end of the street, against the grandiose backdrop of the mountain, the basilica's façade creates an enchanting effect. Its fascination is enhanced by its tall, squared shape, its lively facing of white and pink stone, the perfect proportion of the segments marked out by cornices and pilasters, the airy grace of the deep portals and the rose-windows.

This was the church where, at the end of August, 1294, Fra Pietro Angelerio da Morrone was crowned pope in the presence of cardinals, bishops, princes, and an immense, rejoicing multitude. His could really be called a surprise election, coming at the end of a stormy conclave which had met in Perugia and had dragged on for twenty-seven months because of the irreconcilable hatred between the Orsini and Colonna families, who formed the majority of the Sacred College. The election, considered miraculous, aroused great hopes. The saintly hermit came down from the Morrone, the mountain above Sulmona, riding a donkey and escorted by King Charles d'Anjou and his son Charles Martel, who made a show of protection which Pietro, alas for him, naïvely welcomed. But among those present, expressly summoned by the new pope, there were also the leaders of the semi-clandestine movement, the Spiritual Franciscans, who had been persecuted until then by the ecclesiastical courts for their fierce anti-clericalism, which strictly followed the original rule of Saint Francis. There was also great exultation among the political adversaries of the Church's temporal power, who saw in Celestine the angelic pope, the dove of the Joachimite prophecy. It is not surprising that the pontificate lasted barely a few months and ended in a way unforeseen by canon law.

"Do you realize," my companion said, "that the Church celebrates the date of Celestine's coronation, but not the date of his abdication or his death? Certain fathers of the Council were not wrong when they accused the Church of 'triumphalism'."

"Nevertheless, it's admirable," I answered, "that the Church can even admit scandals and smooth them over."

Stones put up more resistance. The way the original 14th-century basilica, ruined by earthquakes, was restored and subjected to baroque additions is frankly deplorable. Painting, on the other hand, is more docile. In the early days after his canonization, which was fairly prompt, Celestine was often depicted in the act of setting aside his tiara, or actually holding the martyr's palm, an allusion to the legend that he had been murdered by an agent of his successor Boniface VIII, in the fortress of Fumone, where he was a prisoner. Later, the practice of showing him seated on a throne prevailed, and he was called Saint Pier Celestine and not San Pietro Confessore, as canon law would normally have decreed, since at the moment of his death he was no longer pope. This compromise solution inspired an 18th-century bas-relief in the basilica of Santa Maria di Collemaggio, representing Celestine ridding himself of the tiara, illuminated by a ray of light from Heaven. This is the definitive official version, according to which the Holy Spirit intervened twice.

The interior of the basilica, today, was impossible to reach. "We can't let everybody in," a policeman shouted at us. "There's no room." He was forced to raise his voice because of the din made by the bells and the crowd. The vast, jammed square looked like a varicoloured meadow. The women's bright summer blouses and the clergy's white embroidered surplices harmonized happily with the polychrome façade of the basilica. The heat was tempered by a slight breeze which rose, bringing from the nearby fields a pleasant fragrance of mown hay and stubble. The police took advantage of our meekness and energetically pushed us farther and farther back.

"Come on," I said to my friend, annoyed, and we walked along the short path that climbs up the little hill beside the basilica.

"You know what's up here?" he asked me.

"Of course," I answered. "Collemaggio."

In the ordinary speech of the province, the word doesn't denote the church, but the local insane asylum. I still have painful memories of departures, of people leaving our native village for that sad refuge. At one time—I don't know how rightly—the journey was considered a one-way passage. The members of the family witnessed it like a funeral, in which the sick man took part gaily or furiously, according to his condition, while the neighbours spied from behind their doors and windows.

In the porter's lodge we found a rough little old man who, on hearing our names, said he was a companion of mine in remote, elementary-school days. After this recognition, he made a great fuss of me. "At last," he kept saying to me, "at last." He seemed definitely senile, and since we are the same age, he made quite an unpleasant impression on me. He belonged to a peasant family, and I couldn't understand why and how he had left the country for this wretched job. I was about to ask him, but the suspicion that he was a former inmate stopped me.

"Is the ceremony over already?" the old man asked.

"No, but we became bored with it," I answered.

"It's calmer here," he assured me and called an orderly.

I left my friend in the lodge and followed the orderly, looking for the doctor on duty to ask for news about one of the patients. The doctor advised me not to meet him. "He's going through a critical phase," he said, "and he wouldn't even know you." The details he then added about the mental condition of my acquaintance filled me with a sudden, indefinable uneasiness. I left, after a hasty goodbye. To the man from my village I also simply said goodbye. But he didn't want to let me go.

"Do you have permission?" he shouted after me.

As we went down again towards the festive gathering, my friend told me: "The minute we were alone, your fellow-villager confided in me that he has been expecting you to be shut up there for some time now. The delay was incomprehensible to him."

"He thinks I'm crazy?"

"I asked him that and he answered, with assurance: 'If *he* isn't, then who is? He's always been against the government.' It seems that this was the general opinion in your village. But he immediately added that he is fond of you and was waiting for your arrival chiefly so he would have a trusted person to play cards with in his free time. According to him, when you were nine or ten, you played cards with him one Sunday at his house and promised to come back and play every holiday; but you haven't kept your word."

In Celestine's Footsteps

After several days of rain and wind in the Sulmona plain, I woke this morning to find the sky completely clear. A tender gold-green light bathed the fields, the trees, the little villages at the foot of the mountain, and the superb panorama of the Maiella, giving even the slightest object harmonious proportions. Although I was born and brought up in a neighbouring valley, from which the Maiella is invisible, no other mountain touches me as this one does. Complex emotional elements mingle with simple admiration of nature. The Maiella is our holy mountain, here in the Abruzzo. Its spurs, its caves, its passes are charged with memories. Here, where countless hermits once lived, in more recent times hundreds of outlaws have hidden, or escaped prisoners of war, or partisans, many of them helped by the local people.

It would be foolish, perhaps even idolatrous, to consider this passive mountain an agent, connecting such disparate events by its continuity. Still, in their diversity and their heterogeneity, these events illustrate certain constant traits of our mountaineers. The mountain population has often included bizarre individuals who dreamed of some religious or political Utopia, along with the other people who (like the majority of people everywhere) are quite ordinary, simple, taciturn, even crude and mean. When the occasion demands, however, both groups—dreamers and ordinary folk—are capable of exceptional acts of generosity and courage.

When you look at these mountains in this thoughtful mood, it is the figure of Fra Pietro Angelerio that first comes to mind. I am here on his account and I have spent whole days in the archives of the basilica of San Panfilo, studying the numerous documents and relics that concern him. Today I took advantage of the fine weather to go up to the hermitage of Sant'Onofrio, where he had shut himself up when the delegation from the conclave visited him to announce his fatal election. The trip isn't an excursion, but an old-fashioned, sweaty pilgrimage. The new road, flanked by junipers, oaks and beeches, is pleasant, but it didn't take me very far. To go on I was obliged to follow a steep, tortuous path, which in some places forced me to proceed on all fours along the crevices of the rocky cliff. The view from up there was a good excuse to pause and catch my breath. Below, on the slope of the mountain, I saw the ruins of the house of Ovid; farther on, at the beginning of the plain, the vast Abbey of the Holy Spirit; and on the other side the surviving buildings of the former prisoner-of-war camp.

As I proceeded along my path I met an old peasant looking for medicinal herbs, and I stopped to chat with him. He told me that as a young man he went on a pilgrimage to the Holy House in Loreto, and, though I didn't express any doubt of this, he bared one arm to show me the blue tattoo that confirms his journey. He also went on the so-called "pilgrimage of the seven mountains" which originates at the sanctuary of the Trinity, above Subiaco. In the old days, he said, these two pilgrimages were, in the Abruzzo at least, an obligation of conscience for all good Christians. As for San Pier Celestino, or whatever his name is, he's full of respect for him, naturally, but, the old man confided, he has never managed to find out what the saint's specialities are and therefore he has never known how to act: in other words, nobody has ever made it clear to him which are the right graces or favours to pray to the saint for. Celestine can help us—I tried to explain—in avoiding the temptations of power. When the peasant finally understood the meaning of my advice, he was overcome with irrepressible hilarity. Afterwards, he said gravely: "Then he's not a saint for us poor people; he's for the priests."

On returning to the hotel I found the South African poet Uys Krige with his daughter. In addition to the poems in Afrikaans and in English which have won him a reputation as the leading poet of his country, Krige, who is of Boer descent, is also the author of *The Way Out*, which is the most serious and sincere eulogy ever written of the people of these mountains. As a young captain in the South African army, he was taken prisoner in Libya by the Italians and sent to the camp at Sulmona, where he was confined along with several thousand other Allied prisoners.

After the 8th September, 1943, with the passive connivance of the Italian authorities in charge of the camp, all the prisoners escaped and scattered over the nearby mountains, first to evade the round-up which was immediately begun by the Germans and then to cross the line, which at that moment was approaching the Molise. But the undertaking proved far more risky than most of them imagined and it also cost the civilian population sacrifices of every kind.

In his book, Krige simply and movingly narrates countless stories of the spontaneous and courageous solidarity which arose between those poor people and the fugitive prisoners. Before the book appeared, I had already had the opportunity of hearing his verbal account of the events. This was after our first meeting in Rome, towards the end of 1944, when Krige, with tears in his eyes, spoke to me of the shepherds of Roccacasale, of Campo di Giove, of Castel Verrino, of Pietrabbondante, of Cupello. He said without hesitation that the months spent among them were the finest period of his life, since he had glimpsed then, for the first time, the possibility of absolutely pure, selfless human relationships. I have never forgotten some of the stories he told me. I remember one about a farmer of Casa Giovane, on the slopes of the Morrone, who fed and sheltered Krige and two other prisoners for more than a month, even after one wing of the farmhouse had been requisitioned by the Germans. The owner's wife and children consciously shared the danger in this adventure which could have led to their being shot. At one moment, when catastrophe seemed inevitable, as the three men were being searched for, they managed to escape disguised as peasants.

After gaining the slopes of the Monte della Rocca, they reached the village of Roccacasale. Although the place was already crowded with ex-prisoners and there wasn't a single local family that hadn't taken some in, the three men were welcomed with open arms. All the inhabitants, who were very poor, toiled from morning till night to provide decent nourishment for the guests, even as the Germans posted notices on the walls threatening death to anyone who helped escaped Allied prisoners. One day the Germans came with a truck and carried off thirty hostages.

As autumn approached, the first flocks appeared on the meadows of the neighbourhood, migrating towards Apulia. This was the destination the escaping Allied soldiers had in mind. Krige accompanied one of those flocks. It was led by a shepherd who was also its owner, a certain Bartolomeo, who came from the neighbourhood of Teramo and made no difficulties about welcoming Krige. Soon Krige realized that the other men in Bartolomeo's service were, like him, false shepherds. As they continued on their way, they met other flocks with a similar excess of guards; all were heading South.

Once, when they had stopped for the night, near the front, several shepherds came to speak to Bartolomeo. They were profoundly worried. They sat around a great fire where a freshly-skinned lamb was being roasted, and they talked almost the entire night. From a nearby cave Krige, who knew a bit of Italian, was able to follow their conversation.

The shepherds spoke in turn of the imminent danger. Crossing the front line, they said, wouldn't be easy. At night? Impossible, the sheep would scatter, some would fall into ravines and be hurt, the dogs would bark and give the alarm, arouse the attention of the sentries. By day, the situation was even worse: they would surely be sighted by the Germans, who would shoot. The disguise of the ex-prisoners wouldn't deceive anybody; the men were too young and blond and they were obviously gentry, despite their peasant clothes. The shepherds exchanged the latest news of German reprisals against the civilian population. Herds of cattle and flocks of sheep had been confiscated, many families had been shot. The conversation proceeded with long pauses and repetitions of things already said. The arguments all made sense. Krige foresaw the sad, inevitable conclusion, which, however, none of the shepherds dared propose openly. Bartolomeo himself said: "All of you are right. Nobody could blame us." Krige was about to get up and tell the shepherds that he shared their concern; he would assemble the other ex-prisoners in the vicinity and discuss with them how they should face the danger on their own, like soldiers. But Bartolomeo had resumed speaking: "We've brought these men this far," he said, "they're foreigners, they don't know the mountains. How can we abandon them? We're Christians, aren't we?" None of the shepherds made any objection, the migration continued along the established route and they were lucky, since the Germans had evacuated that sector of the front a few hours earlier.

Before leaving Rome in 1945, to go back to South Africa, Krige asked me to witness two vows: he would write a book on the area which he called that "friendly and beloved land'" and as soon as it was possible, he would come back there with his daughter. He was convinced that the girl's education would benefit from knowing those places and those people.

"He was a man of his word," I said to my friend. "There are few who, in peacetime, recall their war-time good intentions."

"If I'm not mistaken," my friend said, "a character in your novel, *A Handful of Blackberries*, found refuge around these parts during the dictatorship, in a Franciscan monastery."

"That's right," I said. "It was old Lazzaro, with his trumpet.'

"The indomitable Lazzaro, with his apocalyptic trumpet," my friend exclaimed. "A Celestinian invention."

"Not entirely an invention," I explained to him. "That trumpet was real. It was an ordinary trumpet which was blown to call the peasants together. Since the majority of them were illiterate, sticking up posters would have been useless. And besides, assembling them by trumpet was the easiest, quickest and cheapest way. During the day the peasants were scattered among the fields, so the trumpet was blown at sunset, when they were on their way home. In a few minutes, the square would fill with people. The peasants would still be carrying on their shoulders the hoes, spades, pickaxes which they had used during the day. They would ask one another in loud voices: 'What is it? What's happened?', since it wasn't possible, by means of the trumpet, to explain in advance the reason for the meeting. Every time, there was a feeling of widespread anxiety, a menacing alarm. There were landowners' families who locked themselves in their houses, barring doors and windows, panic-stricken. With the coming of the dictatorship, the trumpet-blowing was abruptly abolished. The Peasants' League was dissolved, the most active members were outlawed, and the peasants were forbidden to assemble. Obviously the Fascist authorities also searched for the trumpet, in order to confiscate it; but it couldn't be found. The vanished trumpet suddenly became a very important matter. As long as it remained hidden, the power of the dictatorship was precarious. In fact, at the time of the liberation it reappeared."

"A news story that becomes a myth," my friend remarks. "Not an everyday occurrence."

"Yes and no. The trumpet signified the possibility of gathering together. But in certain times and places, the union of the poor assumes an eschatological force."

The Christian Heritage

I continue visiting convents and reading edifying stories. I feel I am now steeped in monkish images of every century, to such a degree that they begin to appear to me in my dreams. I don't find them unpleasant, but for my work, as I now conceive it, they are unnecessary.

During these past few days I've revisited Luco, Trasacco, Ortucchio—ancient towns of the Fucino basin—where I've looked up old friends and I've become convinced that this wandering about is more useful to me than any further research in libraries. I've been led to recall, down to the slightest details, the first time I came to these places as a child, for religious feast-days. The patron saints of these localities are mostly martyrs, conscientious objectors of the first centuries of the Christian era. I couldn't say how far their stories, exalted in panegyrics, affected my thinking. Perhaps even in those days I was beginning to form that vision of my native country and its people which appears in my work. Is it a realistic landscape? I can readily admit it doesn't correspond to the views printed for tourists; and yet it isn't an arbitrary creation.

Actually, in most of the places of the Abruzzo, anyone with an interest in art and the past, after having visited the churches and the convents, finds little or nothing to see. Our local history lacks civic glories comparable to those of other Italian regions. This region was always governed by a capital that lay outside its own boundaries and therefore never had its own court, a lay centre of art and culture. Throughout the Middle Ages and up to the last century, apart from rare exceptions, unusual individuals here found an outlet, a spiritual elevation only in religion.

This region which, because of the harshness of the passes that lead into it and the taciturn nature of its inhabitants, has always been difficult for new beliefs to penetrate, was nevertheless among the first to open itself to Christianity. It was in Apostolic times, when the territory was still the province called Valeria, that Christianity was welcomed here. And the new religion was immediately professed by men who accepted it in all its severity, rejecting the compromises of Constantine, as can be seen in the record of an indigenous monasticism, different from that of Farfa and the Volturno and earlier than the monasticism of Saint Benedict. Those remote beginnings were then destroyed by the extreme violence of the Longobards, but the Abruzzesi's strong ascetic inclination did not die out. In the dark times that followed, it became, in fact, for a considerable number of people, the most accessible form of escape and release from a human condition that was very hard and close to desperation.

Monasticism nevertheless could not prevent the insertion into the parishes' secular life, for most of the faithful, of many pagan myths and customs, symbolic representations of instincts and natural forces. These took root so firmly that they still survive, revealing a special trait of the man of the Abruzzo, who must constantly defend himself against a hostile physical environment.

Numerous monastic communities were formed in the region's mountains, especially in the Maiella district, during the bitter struggles that devastated the land, leaving it prey to conflicts and bandits. Though it avoided open heresy, that flourishing ascetic life remained for a long time outside the official life of the Church, accepting in a free spirit, and at times carrying to extremes, the Benedictine, Joachimite and Franciscan inspirations. Its most conspicuous creation was, in fact, the movement that sprang up in the mid-13th century around the Abbey of the Holy Spirit at Sulmona, inspired by Fra Pietro Angelerio, the future Celestine V. For some time the movement attracted the so-called Spiritual friars, who had broken away from the main body of the Conventual Franciscans. Despite some divergences, the Spiritual friars and Fra Pietro Angelerio's movement were united by a common faith in the imminent Kingdom of God, as it had been announced in the preceding century by Joachim of

Fiore: the expectation of a third age of the human race, the age of the Spirit, without Church, without State, without coercion of any kind, in an egalitarian society, sober, humble, benign, based on man's spontaneous charity.

It isn't possible to understand the period's spiritual crisis and, therefore, the Celestine movement, without going into this basic theme. It is not a question of archaeology or of mere erudition, at least not in our part of the country, for the myth of the Kingdom has never disappeared from Southern Italy, Utopia's chosen home. Even if, in the course of history, Utopia has turned up in our region under other names, there can be no doubt about the idea's continuity.

The history of Utopia, finally, can be set against the official history of the Church and her compromises with the world. It's obvious why the Church, founded juridically and established with all her dogmatic and ecclesiastical apparatus, has always considered with suspicion any revival of the utopian myth. Ever since the Church began to represent herself as the Kingdom, or was so represented by Saint Augustine, she has tried to repress every movement towards a return to primitive belief. Utopia is her bad conscience. The drama of Celestine's predicament for a long period lay in the illusion that the two different ways of following Christ could approach each other and unite. But, when Celestine was forced to choose between them, he didn't hesitate.

This painful laceration of Christianity originated in the fundamental fact that the Kingdom of God, announced by Christ as imminent, had not come about. Nevertheless, some of his meaningful parables, an explicit invocation in the Pater Noster, and repeated admonitions to his disciples confirm it. The Gospel's clear references were afterwards explained by the doctors of the Church in a way consistent with the new situation. Their primitive meaning was, however, not forgotten by everyone, and it has survived at the margins of the Church and sometimes against the Church.

(In quite a different sphere, something similar has happened to Marxism. *The Manifesto of the Communist Party* of 1848 announced an imminent proletarian revolution. Marx, however, had not foreseen that the exploitation of the colonies, which began on a large scale only towards the end of the last century, would provide the great industrial countries with new resources and new markets. The workers' movement consequently fell back, for the most part, on the social-democratic positions of the Second International.)

If the idea of Utopia has not died in religious or political thought it's because Utopia answers a need deeply rooted in man. In man's consciousness there is an unrest that no reform and no material well-being can ever subdue. The history of Utopia therefore is the history of an ever-disappointed, but tenacious hope. No rational criticism can uproot it, and it is important to be able to recognize it even in different guises.

The geology of the Abruzzo, on this score, offers an analogy which I consider worth mentioning if only as an illustration. For many centuries people believed that the Aterno and the Pescara were two different rivers, simply because the Aterno at a certain point vanishes beneath a mountain and the Pescara rises some distance away, apparently "on its own". When the truth was finally suspected, it was easily proved by pouring some coloured matter into the Aterno and waiting until it naturally reappeared in the pseudo-source of the Pescara. To establish the historical continuity of a tendency of the spirit one must obviously resort to less rudimentary research. If it is to be fertile, however, this research must be based not on ideology, but on moral content. As I see it, ideologies only rarely deserve the importance attributed to them. Most of the time they are masks, or alibis, or ornaments. In any case, the spirituality of a serious popular movement is never limited to its ideology, and anyone who wants to form a clear idea of it must not merely observe the movement's banners. Those who agree with this criterion will not think it blasphemous to affirm, for example, that the men who once said "no" to society and went into convents nowadays generally end up among the advocates of social revolution (even if they later deny, or try to deny, their initial impulse).

I have no hesitation in granting rebels the merit of a closer fidelity to Christ. I don't consider myself a missionary, however, but a writer. So I will say frankly that the Christian reality, *hinc et nunc*, seems to me, as a whole, bi-polar, and perhaps it will remain so for some time to come: concordatory and eschatological, historicized and prophetic. Every Christian will continue to find the position that, as a rule, his circumstances assign him, or to make the choice that his conscience dictates.

I have already explained, on another occasion, that for some of us the rediscovery of the Christian heritage remains the most important conquest of the conscience in these past decades. But it isn't, in the sense I have just clarified, an ideological heritage, especially since the ideological element was slight even in our first religious education, to which our families contributed more than priests. Visiting these villages in these past few days, I recalled, among other things, various evangelical parables, apocryphal of course, which I had in fact learned in the family during my childhood and adolescence. The characters, the most famous in the Gospels, were generally seen as natives of this district; and the stories, naturally, were of a moral character, but of a morality not conventional or bigoted: respectful towards Christ and Mary, they displayed a free and sometimes even irreverent attitude towards the apostles, and towards Peter especially, to say nothing of the irreverence towards the civil authorities and their police. An old monk, to whom I told a couple of the parables yesterday, enjoyed them greatly and urged me to write them down. "You could assemble," he said, "an amusing Abruzzese gospel." But that would require textual comparisons and investigations for which I am ill-suited.

Those first rudiments of religious education were complemented, as I have said, by the lives of the first Christian conscientious objectors, and later, by the premature, but not ephemeral experience of the Peasants' Leagues, with which I became associated when I was not yet in high school. This can only apparently be considered political activity. Actually the very word politics fills most poor peasants with disgust.

More than elsewhere, by atavistic tradition they are refractory and distrustful, conceiving of public life as nothing but fraud, theft, and intrigue, no matter who is in power. And they are therefore profoundly sceptical of the possibility of effective democracy and laws applicd cqually to all. The only advantage of a democracy based on popular vote is that the vote, conscientiously used, permits the poor also to share in the intrigue. Then the letter of recommendation—that sacramental document which allows the poor man to make contact with the bureaucracy—costs less and becomes more effective. These prejudices are surely not favourable to the development of free democratic institutions, but it would be a mistake not to examine their historical origin, to consider them simply the product of human wickedness.

At this point a doubt rises in my mind. Haven't I fallen into the error of giving a limited, regional character to the story of Pier Celestine? I may seem to have; but actually I detest regionalism, in which I see only a geographical and administrative value. I believe that most historical differentiations, the most obvious ones, belong to the sphere of manners, and they are generally more marked in the country than in the city. But in fundamental questions there exists, at different levels, a peasant ecumenical spirit which is more substantial and profound than the superficial cosmopolitanism of the guests in grand hotels. Anyone who knows something, if only from books, provided they are authentic books, about the life of the South American *peones*, of the Chinese *coolies*, of the Arab *fellahin*, will easily understand what I mean. Rather than continue this discussion, however, I would like to quote a page from a Polish author, concerning the inhabitants of a remote corner of Siberia. It would be hard to find a region farther removed and more different from ours. The book's author is a former Polish cavalry officer, Slavomir Rawicz, and the book is entitled *The Long Walk*.

The passage was pointed out to me by a friend whom I had told about a Christmas Eve custom in certain parts of Abruzzo, in the days of my childhood. (All during that night the door of the house was left open, the fire kept burning and the table set with food, in case the Holy Family, pursued by Herod's police, had urgent need to hide or refresh themselves.) The passage of the Polish author I have mentioned tells of an incident that took place at the end of January, 1941, when Rawicz and other Polish deportees in Siberia were being transferred from one forced labour camp to another, near Yakutsk. As they proceeded on foot from Irkutsk, their point of departure, after they had crossed the river Lena, a snowstorm forced them to take refuge in a forest for a few days. Since the police vehicles escorting them were unable to follow the deportees into the woods, the commanders rounded up a group of Ostyaks, members of a Mongol race which inhabits the area, with their reindeer and sleds.

The little men, as Rawicz tells the story, arrived with sacks of food and sat with the prisoners around the fire when they received their ration of bread and tea. The Ostyaks looked at the strangers with compassion. Rawicz spoke in Russian with one of them. He must have been about sixty, though with the Mongols it is hard to tell a man's age. Rawicz spoke to him on various occasions. He didn't have much to say. To express an idea he had to think a long time with visible effort. Like all the other Ostyaks, he called the prisoners the "unfortunates". It was an ancient word in their language. From the time of the Tsars, such men had been, to the eyes of that people, the "unfortunates", forced labourers, obliged to extract the riches of Siberia, without wages . . .

"We have always been friends of the 'unfortunates'," the Ostyak said to Rawicz once. "Since long ago, since as far back as memory reaches, before me and before my father, and even before my grandfather and his father, we had the habit of leaving a bit of food outside our doors, for any 'unfortunates' in flight, who had escaped from the camps and didn't know where to go . . ."

Poor, dear, little Ostyaks. It's probable, if not absolutely certain that they have never even heard the names of our villages. But what does that matter? They resemble us like brothers.

What Remains

When a writer who cannot be classified as a bigot or as irreligious starts digging in the subsoil of his native region, rummaging among ancient tales of monks and heretics to find a beloved Utopia, if his friends find out about this activity, he can be sure they will ask him to clarify, in specific terms, his position towards the Church today. This is a request he can hardly avoid, though I don't personally feel it must necessarily be answered. Still, accepting it—or rather, foreseeing it—doesn't disturb me in the least; it's an opportunity to forestall possible misunderstandings.

My position in this matter, I must say first of all, is anything but unusual or exclusive, though it isn't the position of any established group. But, as it is based on a certain personal experience, clarification of it may also be of interest to other people. I'm thinking, in particular, of those who, after having received the usual religious education in some institution or school run by priests, left the Church in their youth, not because of the natural indifference which affects most boys as they reach puberty, or because of intellectual doubts or dissent about the substance of the faith (such cases are rare), but because they could no longer stand the backwardness, the passivity, the conformist behaviour of the clergy in the face of the grave questions imposed by the times. We were, in fact, between seventeen and twenty, at an age which, despite conventional, rhetorical opinion, is the most unhappy in a man's life, and we had to fend for ourselves, one way or another. In that period of maximum confusion, of poverty and social disorder, of betrayal, violence, unpunished crimes and every sort of illegality, the bishops' pastoral letters to the faithful went on discussing, preferably, such themes as women's immodest dress, promiscuous bathing on the beaches, new dances of exotic origin, and traditional bad language. That evasion, on the part of shepherds who had always claimed the moral leadership of their flock, was an intolerable scandal. How could one remain in such a Church?

We will never forget this, not even if we live as long as Methusalah; on the other hand, we cannot remain bound to those old recriminations, while life goes on. Now no one can deny that since then the Church has moved forward. We must say, sincerely, so much the better, and we can only hope that she will persevere in the same direction. The Vatican Council was a positive event which will help everyone, even unbelievers. In the effort made to bring herself up to date and to overcome internal resistance, the Church has shown a spiritual vitality of which many believed her incapable. How can one fail to rejoice? And, further, some of the Council's most courageous decisions contain a satisfactory answer to the questions that formerly were ignored and that led many of us to break away, so we may well repeat: better late than never.

But why do we continue, nevertheless, to remain outside? Allow me to warn the reader that it would be insulting to consider the reason mere pride, vanity or self-interest. We may not be immune to weaknesses of this sort, but they affect other areas. As far as the Faith is concerned, our perplexity has a less trivial explanation. To understand it, we mustn't consider only the initial motive for the break, but we must examine what happens afterwards, in such cases, through the mere fact of breaking away, in the mind of the man who leaves the Church, or any equivalent organization, even a political one. Unless the rebel, as he leaves, falls into a kind of catalepsy, it is inevitable that, as time goes on, the area of his dissent is gradually extended. Why does this happen? Not always and not necessarily because of the bitterness, the resentment, the rancour, the "renegade" feels; but simply because any reality looks different, seen from the outside. Perhaps we haven't given enough thought to the fact that the disciplinary bond and mere physical attendance, even passive, in a community are essential elements in a docile acceptance of common beliefs. I don't mean that, once a man is "outside", religious dogmas seem suddenly artificial and arbitrary to him. No, they do not immediately lose their prestige, their fascination, their plausibility; but sooner or later, they show themselves for what they are: the exclusive truths of the Church, her spiritual patrimony, what distinguishes her from other Churches, including other Christian ones; in a word, her ideology. No longer, therefore, the message of the Father to His children, to all His children, the clear natural light discovered at birth, the common weal, universal, manifest truth, irresistible to any intelligence in good faith; instead we see a complex historical product, the product of a given culture, or rather the amalgam of various cultures, the millennial elaboration by a closed community, in constant inner turmoil and also in competition and conflict with others. Finally, to put it charitably: a noble, a venerable superstructure. But what happens to poor Christ in such a superstructure?

Ingenuousness, once lost, is naturally hard to recover, and it cannot even be decently regretted. Can it be simulated? After having lived through the loss of innocence, to go back and pretend to accept a system of dogmata whose validity is no longer recognized as absolute would be to suppress reason, to violate one's conscience, to lie to oneself and others, to insult God. No one can ask that of us; no flattery or violence, no well-intentioned pressure can impose it on us. Fortunately, Christ is greater than the Church.

I have already indicated that something of the sort can happen to the man who leaves a political party whose structure resembles that of the Church, a closed society, as is the case of the Communist Party. After what has already been said, a single example is enough. Those who left the Communist Party after the 'thirties, because they rejected the stupid Stalinist theory of Social-Fascism and its infamous corollary, according to which the destruction of democratic institutions by Nazism was a step forward in the proletarian emancipation, did not at that moment reject the rest of Communist theory and practice. On the contrary, they nourished the illusion that they were still quite orthodox. But, some twenty years later, when the 20th Congress of the Soviet Communist Party condemned Stalinism and some of its most evil aberrations, blaming them on the so-called "personality cult", those former party members did not feel there was any question of their returning to the fold. Why not? Hadn't the 20th Congress been, in its way, a step forward? No doubt it had, but for some time, such men had no longer considered themselves Communists. Being "outside", away from the intellectual influence of the closed society and breathing free air, their first, limited dissent had gradually extended to apply to the whole 19th-century pseudo-scientific framework of Leninism, with its totalitarian practice.

What remains in the mind, when one does not belong to any Church or party, cannot be declared in the form of a credo with articles. As far as I am concerned, I consider myself, in spite of everything, a Christian and a Socialist. In any case, I attach no importance to labels. The first Christians were considered atheists by some people simply because they refused to follow the conventional forms of religious observance. If I were to follow their example and declare publicly, for example, what I think of the ritual of laying wreaths on the tomb of the Unknown Soldier, our so-called "altar of the fatherland", I would probably risk arrest for public defamation.

What remains then is a Christianity without myths, reduced to its moral essence, and a great respect but very little nostalgia for what has been lost along the way. What else? After careful consideration, and in order to omit nothing, I might also say: there remains the *Pater Noster*. In the Christian sense of fraternity and an instinctive devotion to the poor, there also survives, as I have said, the loyalty to socialism. I am well aware that this term is now used to mean the most odd and contradictory things; so I am forced to add that I use it in the most traditional sense: an economy in the service of *man*, not of the State or of any policy of power.

THE STORY OF A HUMBLE
CHRISTIAN

THE CHARACTERS

Fra Pietro Angelerio (Celestine V, Pier Celestine)
Matteo da Pratola, *weaver*
Concetta, *his daughter*
Don Costantino, *pastor of Sulmona*
Cerbicca, *a poor man of various trades*
Fra Bartolomeo da Trasacco
Fra Angelo da Caramanico
Fra Tommaso da Sulmona
Fra Ludovico da Macerata } *Morronese monks*
Fra Berardo da Penne
Fra Tommaso da Atri
Fra Clementino da Atri
Cardinal Benedetto Caetani (Boniface VIII)
The Military Adjutant of King Charles II of Naples
The Secretary of Celestine V
Gioacchino } *Neopolitan clerks, then*
Luca } *Morronese novices*
The Bailiff of Sulmona
A Gendarme
A Messenger of the Bishop, a young Morronese monk, some prelates, a group of poor people

I

Sulmona, May 1294

A secluded little square in Sulmona, at the foot of Monte Morrone. From a broad staircase in the rear rise the low, uneven walls of a church under construction; work on the building, however, seems to have stopped years before. On the left side of the square there is a small shrine with a sacred image, an oil lamp burning before it. On the right, a humble, one-storey house, the dwelling and workshop of a family of artisans, a weaver and his daughter. The house has a broad doorway and a window protected by an iron grille. At eye-level some wooden stakes are fixed into the walls, for hanging up work; for the same purpose, next to the door, there is a wooden saw-horse which can be shifted as desired. A rarely-used street, which links the square with the centre of the little city, passes in front of the steps.

It is dawn. After a few seconds, during which the stage is deserted, a young woman appears at the already-open door of the weaver's house. This is Concetta. *In her arms she is carrying some bundles of red wool which she hangs on the pegs by the door. She is dressed in black, very simply, according to the custom of poor women of the artisan class on working days. She wears no hat and her hair is arranged in the traditional manner, gathered in a little bun at the nape. She wears slippers of dark cloth. She is a pleasant-looking girl of about twenty-five, sturdy, a bit rustic, shy but not servile. After looking to left and right, she advances timidly towards the audience.*

CONCETTA: Good evening, all. It will probably seem strange to you that the first explanation of this story which is about to begin—and which is a story about men—should be given you by a woman, and an ordinary woman like me, a weaver.

I don't mind telling you it seems strange to me, too. But the author, for some reason of his own, chose to do it this way. So I must ask you to be patient with me if I am too simple. This is a story about men, as I said before: men quarrelling among themselves; men of the church, arguing about how to interpret the Gospel and the Rule laid down by Saint Francis just a few dozen years ago. Sometimes they actually come to blows, they hit one another with sticks, and excommunicate one another. Even a calm, honest man like my father is so upset by it all that it's pitiful. He receives odd visits, and for a while, if I went up to him when he was talking with strangers, he would say: "Concetta (Concetta is my name), go in the other room, please", or else he would just motion me away. Mind you, it never occurred to me that they might be discussing wicked or dishonest things. God be thanked, my father isn't capable of that.

But from various clues, and especially because I sometimes saw one or two monks among the strangers, the kind they now call Zealots or Spiritual friars, I finally guessed that my father was involved in church questions. I asked myself: why all the mystery then? Religion concerns women at least as much as it does men. So one day, partly joking, and partly to lead him on, I said to my father: "I've heard tell there was a time when they thought women had no soul; have you begun to suspect that, too?" I should never have taken such a liberty; he was really offended. Now I needn't stand here and tell you all the words he used to answer my reproach. "I only wanted to spare you suffering," he said finally, to justify what he had done. "But, since you ask me, I'll gladly tell you everything."

Now I have to admit that the dear man, as far as my suffering was concerned, had been right. Even if I try to hide it, now that he's told me about the disagreements and the fights between the so-called Spiritual Franciscans and the others, the Conventuals, my heart is filled with anguish. However, I'm not sorry I insisted on knowing the truth.

First of all, it's a question of conscience: my father's a widower, and every daughter will understand me when I say I couldn't leave him alone, to face any troubles that might come up. And besides, how can a good Christian girl be indifferent to the sufferings of the Church?

But I'm also tormented by the fear of accepting mistaken ideas. So, a few days ago, to set my conscience at rest, I went with another girl—a friend of mine—to talk to our pastor, Don Costantino. To tell the truth, it was the pastor himself who sent for us, for another reason. I don't know whether to tell you about it or not. Well, perhaps I should, just in a few words, especially since this other story also has a slight sequel. What had happened was this: we girls in the Sodality of the Daughters of Mary came to an agreement and for a couple of Sundays we haven't been to the High Mass at noon, which is also called the nobility's Mass, and instead we've gone to the Low mass at five in the morning. This change didn't go unnoticed, because the place reserved for us girls was right in the church's centre aisle, in front of everybody, near the altar rail, with the raised pews of the gentry to our right and left. So, one Sunday recently, when the church was crowded for the noon Mass, our place was unexpectedly empty. And the same the following Sunday. The nobles, who apparently don't have an easy conscience, took offence, and one of them, a baron well-known both for his wicked actions and for his many generous gifts to the church, went and complained to the bishop. In fact, it seems that the nobleman had been talking with his informers, so he blamed me and my friend for having arranged the insult.

"Would you mind telling me," the pastor asked us, putting on a stern face, "why you don't turn up for the noon Mass on Sunday any more, and why you go to the five o'clock Mass instead?"

"We thought," I said to him, "that at five in the morning Our Heavenly Father is already awake. Were we wrong?"

The pastor burst out laughing, and, since he knows the

real reason for our behaviour as well as we do, and in his heart he approves of it, he didn't insist. All he said was: "I'll settle matters with the bishop, but what about the baron and the other nobles? May the Madonna protect you."

After he had said this, we could have left; but since we were there, we begged Don Costantino to explain to us the quarrel that's come up in the Church and especially among the Franciscans. We were surprised to see that this question caused him great embarrassment: he had a terrible fit of coughing. Finally, since he's an educated man, he tried to get out of it with a few remarks that were neither fish nor fowl. "There are devout persons," he said, "who read the Holy Scriptures in different ways. Some read them forwards, and some backwards, or a little crooked, or sideways."

"Couldn't the book be held still?" we suggested, following his own way of talking. "Couldn't the Holy Scriptures be nailed to a desk or a wall?"

"That would be of no use, because it doesn't depend on the book; it depends on the reader. There are some who see things backwards, and others a bit crooked."

We insisted; we couldn't believe it was impossible to find a solution. "Couldn't they take the book away," we suggested, "from those who see it crooked?"

The pastor shook his head. "How can you tell who they are?" he said. "Each insists it's the other who is reading backwards."

At this point, to put an end to all this beating about the bush, I had an idea. "Still there's the pope," I said. "Isn't the pope over everybody?"

The good pastor, at that, heaved a deep sigh. "The last pope died more than two years ago," he told us, "and since then the Cardinals have been meeting in a conclave, first in Rome, and now, because of the heat, in Perugia, but they can't come to an agreement and elect a new one."

"In two years they haven't been able to agree?" I

couldn't help exclaiming. "But doesn't the Holy Spirit dictate the choice of the pope? You taught us that in catechism class."

"Yes, it's the Holy Spirit," he said. "But apparently the cardinals are turning a deaf ear."

"If those cardinals can't hear, they should make some new ones," my friend blurted out at once. "They should make some others with good hearing. How can you leave the Church for years without a pope?"

"Only the pope can appoint new cardinals," the priest answered us patiently.

"Why doesn't he appoint them? Why doesn't he hurry?" we answered without stopping to think.

Then the pastor lost his patience. "He doesn't appoint them because there isn't any pope," he shouted. "The throne is vacant, I've told you that already. For two years we've been without a pope . . ."

We apologized for our muddled heads, and the pastor, as if repenting that he had raised his voice, walked to the door with us.

We were disappointed. After all that talk we still hadn't got anywhere. But, to our surprise, the last words we exchanged, at the door of the sacristy, held out a ray of hope.

"This old hermit of Monte Morrone, the one they talk so much about . . . they even say he's worked various miracles," I said, "this Fra Pietro—whose side is he on?"

At that, the old pastor's face brightened. "He's a good man, as pure as spring water," he told us. "He's a true Christian like those of the days of the Apostles. Do you know him?" he asked.

We had to admit we had seen him only once, from a distance, because he won't allow women near him.

"Every now and then he changes his place of refuge, to evade those who want to disturb him. Luckily for him, Divine Providence has furnished our mountains, the Morrone and the Maiella, with many caves. But to answer your question," the priest added, turning to me, "well, I can tell you that Fra Pietro is above all quarrels. Naturally he too has his preferences, he protects the Spirituals, considering them closest to the teaching of Saint Francis, but he's respected by everyone."

"If that's so," my friend said impulsively, "why don't they make him pope?"

At those words, the good old man raised his arms towards heaven and for a long time he didn't breathe a word. "If only they would," he grumbled. "It wouldn't be against Canon Law, after all; but the cardinals prefer to appoint one of their own number." Then he added, in a low voice, as if talking to himself: "It would take a direct intervention of the Holy Spirit, the Holy Spirit would have to descend on the Roman Curia."

"If the Holy Spirit really cares about his Church," I couldn't help saying then, "he ought to allow himself a little thing like that."

At those words, the pastor abruptly changed expression. "Go away, temptresses," he ordered. Then he added, smiling: "You have poor judgement, but you're rich in faith."

After that we came home, as you can well imagine, more upset than before. Surely these are confused and difficult times for humble Christians. Forgive me for all this chatter. This is how our story begins.

[*As Concetta is saying these last words, her father, Matteo, appears at the door of the house, observing her with amusement and surprise.*]

MATTEO: Concetta, what are you doing? Talking to the birds?
CONCETTA (*runs towards him*): I wish I had been.

[*Matteo doesn't insist; he seems to have other things on his mind. He is an elderly man, tall and thin, dressed humbly, but in a clean and seemly fashion. His head is bare, his wide-sleeved cotton blouse is open at the neck; his trousers come to his knees; he wears rope-soled clogs on his feet.*]

MATTEO: This is going to be a hard day. Will you be able to finish that blanket for the girl who's being married tomorrow?

CONCETTA: It's almost finished. I wasn't able to sleep last night, so I got up and went on with it. Didn't the noise of the loom wake you?

MATTEO: I sleep like a rock, you know that. But you, daughter, are ruining your health. You work too much and you eat like a sparrow.

CONCETTA: While I was sleeping I had a frightful vision. A huge, black wolf, with his jaws open wide, and his eyes blazing, was standing there—just over there, halfway down the steps—and he was looking at our door. I woke up with a start, as you can imagine. My heart was pounding, I recited a *Pater* and I tried to go back to sleep. But as soon as I closed my eyes, that awful animal came back. Tell me, what can it mean? Is it a warning? Of what? I don't know, but I knew the only way to be rid of it was to get up and go to my loom.

MATTEO (*looks at her, touched*): Perhaps you think too much.

CONCETTA: But I promise you: they aren't bad thoughts. Well, we mustn't waste time, and to keep that beast away, let's start working. I need a few spools for the shuttles, and if you have time, you should try to repair the winder. It won't turn.

[*The dialogue between father and daughter continues as, each on his own, they set to work. Matteo brings the winder out from the house, places it beside the door and starts repairing it. At the same time, Concetta unwinds the thread from one of the skeins hung on the wall and winds it around a little spool.*]

CONCETTA: Aren't you expecting some of those friars to come today, the ones they call the Spirituals?

MATTEO: I was just thinking about them. But I don't know what time they'll arrive.

CONCETTA: Will there be many of them?

MATTEO: I don't know. You never can tell. I'm sure there'll be a couple from Macerata, which is one of their most active centres. But others may join them along the way.

CONCETTA: Will they come all the way from Macerata to Sulmona on foot? The poor things will be exhausted when they reach here.

MATTEO: Certainly, if they didn't have a great faith sustaining them, only a few, the youngest, would survive. Just think of the hardship of those long stretches of mountain, the storms, which are so frequent this time of year, and the scarcity—or total lack—of food. Not to mention the persecution of the authorities, especially in some dioceses of the Papal States. Every now and then some of the best-known friars are put in prison.

CONCETTA: They're not criminals, after all!

MATTEO: They are in the eyes of some authorities, and criminals of the worst sort: they're considered heretics.

CONCETTA (*alarmed*): Real heretics?

MATTEO: Not as far as the principles of Christian faith are concerned, not at all. No more than Saint Francis was, and they consider themselves his most faithful disciples. (*Matteo examines the sky.*) You see those clouds over the Pescara, towards Penne? If they bring rain, the men will be late.

CONCETTA: Will these friars stay with us for a long time?

MATTEO: Long enough to take some refreshment and put themselves in touch with Fra Pietro.

CONCETTA: That won't be easy, I'm afraid. For some while now nobody's known where Fra Pietro has taken refuge.

MATTEO: The Abbot of the Holy Spirit will know at least, and I've sent him word by Fra Bartolomeo da Trasacco. You know him, too. He is one of the most respected monks, one of Fra Pietro's first companions.

CONCETTA: But if these friars of Macerata are coming here to talk with Fra Pietro, and, as you say, he is happy to see them, why don't they take shelter in his abbey?

MATTEO: They hate the big convents. I thought I explained that to you. In fact, this is one of the main points of their disagreement with the other Franciscans, and for this same reason, in spite of their devotion to Fra Pietro, they won't join his congregation. Once when I accompanied them to the abbey, they caused a very unpleasant stir among the monks. They say that the big convents inevitably create a spirit of regimentation and become centres of power and wealth, contradicting the true Christian spirit. So they prefer small, free communities, temporary settlements, without any possessions.

CONCETTA: Forgive me if I ask an indiscreet question, father. Do you agree with everything about these Spiritual friars?

MATTEO: Well, not everything perhaps. If I agreed with them completely, I wouldn't lead a family life.

CONCETTA (*warmly*): Father, I wouldn't like to be an obstacle to your vocation.

MATTEO: I know that, my dear, don't worry. Even in matters of the spirit, you're always a help to me, never an obstacle. But, while we're on the subject, I want to be completely sincere with you. My education is limited, you know, so I can't understand everything. The main reason I help these friars is, after all, quite simple; it's because they are persecuted for questions of conscience. Besides, Fra Pietro himself, the last time I met him, urged me specifically to do it.

[*Concetta smiles. Fra Pietro's approval is a great relief to her.*]

CONCETTA: I've been worrying about how to feed these poor men when they arrive. These are things we women must take care of, aren't they? Did you see the kettle of beans by the fireplace? They're already cooked and can be heated up in a moment. Unfortunately, they're all we have left. We also have a couple of onions, and in the bread-bin there's a dish of rye flour and half a loaf. I'm afraid that, for these starving men, this will just arouse their appetite, and not satisfy it.

MATTEO: I've tried to think of some friend we could ask for help, even a loan, but nobody has come to mind. Such hard times have never been known before, around here. I've heard of entire families of artisans ill because they have to live on grass and leaves, like animals.

CONCETTA: You know we had to give our last bit of money to the spinning-mill, as an account on our old debt. Otherwise they won't give us any more wool. And the girl who is coming this evening to collect her blanket frankly warned us ahead of time that she wouldn't be able to pay promptly. What will we do if the friars we're expecting are numerous? And if they stay here tomorrow as well? That's why I . . .

MATTEO: God will provide. But you had something else to say.

CONCETTA: After thinking about this, I decided yesterday evening to speak with the pastor, Don Costantino. I told him at once I hadn't been sent by you and I was speaking on my own. A woman is allowed to ask for charity. Father, why are you looking at me like that? Have I done something wrong?

MATTEO (*with unusual harshness*): Very wrong.

CONCETTA (*upset, but ready to defend herself*): I didn't ask anything for us, or anything from his own pocket. Everyone knows that the parish has some income; as a member of the parish I think that income should be used in situations like this, when private charity isn't enough. Feeding the hungry is one of the corporal works of mercy.

MATTEO: Another thing that isn't listed among the works of mercy, but should be, is not to betray the persecuted.

CONCETTA (*with great surprise*): Betray? Father, do you think that's the right word? Please, don't speak in anger.

MATTEO (*still harsh*): I repeat: Don Costantino is not a person to be trusted.

CONCETTA (*looks around to make sure no one is approaching the square, then gives her protest free rein*): Not trust our pastor? Well, you're a little late in telling me. Didn't you allow him to baptize me? And when I want to go to confession, he's the one I turn to. And at Easter both of us receive Holy Communion from him. He tended my mother on her

deathbed, and you were the one who went to call him. Isn't
that enough?

MATTEO (*irked*): I know, I know, but I'm not talking about his
qualities as a priest, the power given him, by Holy Orders,
to administer the sacraments. I'm talking about his
behaviour towards the Spiritual friars. He's not to be
trusted, I say; he's a coward. You still haven't told me how
he answered your plea for help.

CONCETTA (*suddenly seized with the suspicion that she acted hastily,
almost stammering*): He said that he wasn't, you might say,
personally opposed. But then he said that, as pastor, he
was obliged—or maybe he used another word, I don't
remember—obliged to ask the opinion, or else the authorization, of the bishop. Forgive me, father, I have a bad
headache.

MATTEO (*heedless of his daughter's complaint, with unrelenting
harshness*): You see? Since when has a special permission
been necessary for works of mercy? Aren't they a duty
towards everyone, even unbelievers?

CONCETTA: An ordinary Christian surely doesn't need permission, but Don Costantino is a priest and perhaps he
has to be more careful.

MATTEO (*as before*): What else did he say to you?

CONCETTA (*downcast*): He asked me if I knew the name of any of
the friars that were coming.

MATTEO: Why did he want to know that, unless it was to
denounce them? Did you ask him why? If you want to give
a crust of bread to someone in need, do you have to know
his name?

CONCETTA (*exhausted, tries to minimize the gravity of her mistake*):
The worst that can happen is that the bishop will refuse his
authorization.

MATTEO: No, my child, that would be the best that could
happen. The worst might be something else: the bishop
might insist that the civil authorities arrest the friars. He
has all the legal pretexts he needs. To condemn the
innocent, men in command can always find some law.

They make the laws. In this way, our humble home, which was to be a place of friendly repose for those poor friars, risks becoming a trap.

[*Concetta can no longer restrain her sobs. She covers her face with her hands and escapes into the house. Matteo, also depressed and concerned, carries the winder inside, along with the little skeins that had been hanging on the walls.*]

CHRISTIAN OUTLAWS IN SEARCH OF ASYLUM

When the little square is empty, the first of the friars, Fra Ludovico, arrives from the left. Sweaty and dusty, he is a man of about forty, wearing a habit of undyed wool, bound at the waist by a rope. His beard is two weeks old. Though he is in bad shape, he is not unseemly, nor is there anything "theatrical" about him. His expression is that of a cultivated, tenacious man. He bows briefly at the shrine and makes a slow turn about the square, reconnoitring. When Matteo appears at the door of the house, the friar comes over to him with a smile.

FRA LUDOVICO: Does a weaver live or work around here, a certain Matteo da Pratola?

MATTEO (*delighted*): I'm Matteo. Have you come from Macerata?

FRA LUDOVICO: Yes, I'm Fra Ludovico. Long live Saint Francis.

MATTEO: Long live Saint Francis. Are you alone?

FRA LUDOVICO: Six brothers are with me. We had to leave two others behind on the road, ill. On the road is the right expression. We tried to find haven for them in a hospice, but we had no luck.

[*From the corner of the street where he arrived, Fra Ludovico now motions to the other brothers, who have been waiting.*]

MATTEO: Did you have other mishaps during your journey?

FRA LUDOVICO: At Ascoli we were questioned for a long time by a stupid, pompous gendarme. Not knowing what line to take, he told us to wait while he ran to the bishopric. Go, go, we said to him, we're in no hurry. Naturally, when he left, we also took our leave.

MATTEO: There may be some complications here, too, I'm afraid.

FRA LUDOVICO (*smiling*): Complications don't frighten us. As we say in our parts, if Christ were afraid of mice, he wouldn't stay in church.

MATTEO: Still, we must think about some avenue of escape. (*The two men confer in low voices.*) You had better tell the others too, as soon as they arrive.

[*A moment later, two elderly friars appear, Fra Berardo da Penne and Fra Tommaso da Atri, and behind them, toying with a long leafy branch, Fra Clementino, who also comes from Atri. He is no more than a boy. They are all dressed in the same way, in a rough woollen habit, tied at the waist by a cord, barefoot or with their feet bound in rags. Still, the striking thing about them is not the oddness of their dress but their serious, stubborn, even slightly disturbing expression. Fra Berardo and Fra Tommaso are artisans, Fra Clementino a student. Passing the shrine, the three bow. Fra Clementino lingers there, to stick his leafy bough into the grating that protects the shrine.*]

FRA CLEMENTINO (*inspired, both in his gesture and in the sound of his voice*):
> Oh, son, oh son, oh son of God.
> Celestial flower, celestial food.

(*He turns to the older friars, already seated, scattered over the steps of the church*): We must write to Todi, to our Fra Jacopone, and ask him to compose a special hymn for us, to keep our spirits up when we're on the road.

FRA BERARDO: Yes, and to protect us from rain and hunger.

FRA TOMMASO: And to keep flies away from us, and mad dogs and police spies.

MATTEO: You must want to wash. There's a stream behind the house. I'll take you there at once, but first I'll fetch some cloths for you to dry yourselves with.

[*Matteo goes into the house and comes out with two white cloths; after a moment's reflection, he shuts the door; the four friars follow him behind the house.*

As soon as they have disappeared, a gendarme arrives from the right. He has a long sabre and the arrogant manner of the minor officials of the southern provinces. He takes a turn around the square and stops at the window, which is still open.]

GENDARME (*in a loud voice*): Matteo . . . Matteo . . . Nobody home?

CONCETTA (*from within*): My father's not home.

GENDARME: Did some strange friars arrive here, just a little while ago?

CONCETTA (*within*): You can ask my father that.

GENDARME: There's something I can ask you, too. Do you have an innkeeper's licence? No, you don't; only a weaver's. You and your father are weaving some odd cloth nowadays. Poor as you are, why do you want to make trouble for yourselves?

CONCETTA (*just inside the grille at the window*): We accept no recompense from pilgrims, so we are not innkeepers. Hospitality is a work of mercy.

GENDARME: I see you have a ready tongue. So perhaps you'll have an explanation for the insult you organized, against the baron. I mean the insult in church, which everybody is talking about.

CONCETTA: Our pastor, Don Costantino, can answer that question for you. He's in charge of church matters.

GENDARME: In other matters, however, the bailiff is in command. And he was the one who sent me here.

[*The gendarme retraces his steps and disappears.*

Immediately afterwards, Matteo returns and, following him, the friars, one by one. They sit down again on the steps of the church. Only Fra Clementino remains standing, like a child who can't restrain his restlessness.]

FRA LUDOVICO: Sit down, my boy; aren't you tired, too?

FRA CLEMENTINO: On the contrary. When I think that we're at the foot of the Morrone, not far from Fra Pietro, I have to control myself, to keep from turning handsprings.

FRA TOMMASO: Don't be boastful. Boastfulness is unseemly in a friar. Admit that you, too, are tired. (*Brusquely, in a defiant tone.*) Are you able to jump over that sawhorse?

FRA CLEMENTINO: Certainly, what do you want to bet?

FRA LUDOVICO: My boy, remember this once and for all: a friar doesn't make bets.

FRA CLEMENTINO (*pretends not to have heard*): Will you bet your share of the metal button we found together, on the road, which is our common property, undivided and indivisible?

FRA LUDOVICO: Property? Now you're really talking like a Conventual.

FRA CLEMENTINO: Very well, I'll renounce the prize. Glory will be enough for me.

[*There is silence for the test. The young friar measures the obstacle a couple of times, withdraws to the right distance for a running start, bursts forth and then runs around the sawhorse, causing general laughter.*]

FRA CLEMENTINO: What's there to laugh about? Wasn't the important thing to pass the obstacle?

[*Finally he too goes and sits down. Matteo, uneasy, shifts constantly from one spot to another, to keep watch on the streets leading into the square. Meanwhile, Concetta comes out of the house with a rough trencher, three bowls and a cup, all filled with bean soup, and two spoons. The girl's eyes are still red from weeping, but she makes an effort to seem at ease. The friars stand up to pray.*]

FRA LUDOVICO: Benedicite, Domine.

[*The rest of the prayer is spoken in a murmur. After it, the friars sit down again.*]

MATTEO: This is my daughter. Her name is Concetta.

CONCETTA (*serving the friars*): I'm sorry, we have only two spoons. But, anyway, you've washed your hands. I'll give the spoons to the oldest, is that right?

FRA BERARDO: To tell the truth, we've also washed our faces and our feet.

FRA CLEMENTINO: Yes, if it doesn't seem boastful—even our feet. But as a rule we use our hands for eating. I must tell you, Mistress . . .

CONCETTA: I'm not your mistress, but your servant.

FRA LUDOVICO: In our Father's house there are no masters, mistresses or servants, but only children, all free and equal.

FRA CLEMENTINO: Well, daughter, your beans smell delicious, so delicious I'm afraid of committing a sin of gluttony.

CONCETTA: I seasoned them only with herbs gathered on the Morrone.

FRA CLEMENTINO: Then there can be no sin, am I right, Fra Ludovico? Because the Morrone is purified by the presence of the holy hermits. In any case, to thank you, I want to teach you a secret that might be very useful to you in the future. Watch carefully. (*He goes to the girl and with a length of string, he performs—for her and for the audience— the trick of the false hangman's knot, winning easy exclamations of surprise from the girl.*) Here is the secret: now pay close attention. (*He reveals it simply.*) So, if the art of the loom should one day go out of style—alas, the fate of all human things—you can go about the world, in cities and villages, performing this trick. I assure you, you'll earn good money.

CONCETTA (*going along with the joke*): But I wouldn't know what to do with so much money.

FRA CLEMENTINO: You can always donate it to a convent of Franciscans.

[*Concetta laughs, collects the vessels and the spoons on the board, and takes them back into the house.*]

THE SCANDAL OF THE CONCLAVE

Matteo returns to his guard duty, and soon he takes a huge hand-kerchief from his pocket, and waves it towards Fra Ludovico, without saying a word. Fra Ludovico realizes this is an alarm signal. Three friars, Fra Berardo, Fra Tommaso and Fra Clementino, hastily climb the steps and disappear behind the walls, while Fra Ludovico remains seated where he is, and Matteo pretends to be busy moving the sawhorse. From the street that leads into the square at the right Don Costantino appears. The pastor is an elderly man, kindly-looking, paternal.

DON COSTANTINO (*surprised to see Matteo doesn't greet him and even turns his back, and surprised, too, at finding only one friar; after a long silence he addresses Fra Ludovico*): Peace be with you . . . I'm the pastor of that church you see over there. Where have your companions gone? Have they hidden?

FRA LUDOVICO: Unfortunately, a priest's cassock doesn't inspire trust.

DON COSTANTINO: I'm sorry. What must I do to overcome your distrust? Only a little while ago I said Mass and I asked the Lord to inspire your hearts towards a friendly meeting.

FRA LUDOVICO: I must warn you at once, father: have no illusions. If this were a matter of personal resentment, of private wrongs or offence, well, then it would be easy: I would be the first to kneel before you and ask your forgiveness. But you and I don't know each other, and there are no personal quarrels between us. What there is, instead, is the abyss dug by the degeneration of your Church and by the betrayal of the spirit of Saint Francis on the part of many who take his name. This betrayal was made possible with the help of the pope, the bishops, and priests.

DON COSTANTINO: Do you think it's impossible for us even to speak with each other?

[*Matteo sets the sawhorse against the wall and leans or sits on it, whichever is more comfortable, so that he can follow the discussion. At the same time Concetta appears at the grille of the window, her hands joined in the attitude of prayer.*]

FRA LUDOVICO: Come to the point, father, let's not waste time. Are you here of your own free will, or were you sent here?

DON COSTANTINO: Both. I myself asked the bishop to send me here rather than anyone else. Your encounter with another person would surely have been more severe.

FRA LUDOVICO: And therefore quicker. What mission was given you?

FRA CLEMENTINO (*appears between two sections of wall, at the top of the steps, and remains there a short time, long enough to recite, with slightly declamatory gestures and voice, some verses of a sacred laud*):

As four winds move the sea,
So four winds move the mind:
In fear and hope live we,
By joy and sorrow bound.

DON COSTANTINO (*after having observed the youth, Fra Clementino, with curiosity, addresses Fra Ludovico*): I'm sorry I have to begin at once with painful questions. Obviously, my faith in your sincerity can be taken for granted. I am, then, charged to ask if there are any escaped prisoners among you or anyone wanted by an ecclesiastical court.

FRA LUDOVICO (*springs to his feet, filled with indignation, and goes to the pastor, who draws back, frightened*): Did you say that you just celebrated the Holy Mass? And you can transform yourself into a spy so quickly?

DON COSTANTINO (*profoundly embarrassed*): My task—I know—is unpleasant, but I accept it and I must carry it out and not let myself be intimidated (*catches his breath*). You must tell me at least if Pietro da Fossombrone is in your company.

FRA LUDOVICO (*who was going back to the steps, turns at the name and cries out*): Are you seeking Pietro da Fossombrone? You know who he is? And you dare name him without covering your face in shame? For seventeen years you kept that wonderful Christian in a vile prison, then you exiled him to Cilicia, only because with his words and his writings he was spreading the true teaching of Saint Francis, and now you are hounding him again.

[*Drawn by the wrathful voice of Fra Ludovico, the other three friars, who had first hidden behind the walls, now appear at the top of the steps.*]

DON COSTANTINO (*exhausted, on the point of collapsing*): It seems that Pietro da Fossombrone has returned secretly to Italy and is once more conspiring against the Church. Personally I can say only this: I hope he isn't among you.

FRA LUDOVICO: He was initiated in the knowledge of Saint Francis's authentic teaching, by the saint's most loyal and beloved disciple, Frate Leone. This is why you hate him and persecute him like a bandit.

[*Fra Berardo and Fra Tommaso come down the steps together and take their place beside Fra Ludovico. Fra Clementino, instead, remains on the last step, smiling and shifting from one side to the other, with irregular movements, as if dancing, while he looks up at the sky. Don Costantino can't stand up any longer; he goes and sits where Fra Ludovico was seated before. The monks turn on him.*]

FRA BERARDO (*to the pastor*): You priests make us homesick for the days of Nero and Diocletian. To be persecuted by those declared enemies of Christ must have been less painful.

FRA TOMMASO: Hatred among brothers—nothing is more cruel.

DON COSTANTINO (*defends himself weakly*): Mind you, that statement applies also to you, Zealot friars.

FRA LUDOVICO (*to his brothers, pointing to the priest*): He's the pastor of that church over there. The bishop sent him to look for us, to question us like a police informer.

FRA BERARDO (*to the pastor*): His Excellency, your bishop, I imagine, also wears a great gold cross on his chest, hanging from a fine gold chain.

FRA TOMMASO (*with open sarcasm*): Cross and chain, I suppose, are of pure gold. Gold, I might say, like that golden calf in the Bible. In fact, that famous calf was undoubtedly also of finest gold.

DON COSTANTINO (*shrugs, annoyed*): Your criticism is ridiculous, infantile, demagogic. For your information, our bishop is a very worthy man. It is not mere love of pomp that makes him wear certain ritual ornaments; he is simply living up to the dignity of his office. (*The friars surround him and vie with one another in rejecting his reasons.*)

FRA LUDOVICO (*to the pastor*): The cross of Christ, if I'm not mistaken, was made of wood, and so are most of the crucifixes you see now, both in churches and outside them. Do you think that for this reason they lack dignity?

FRA BERARDO (*to the pastor*): Do you believe that if Christ had gone about Palestine with a mitre or a triple crown on his head, he would have been more dignified?

FRA LUDOVICO (*to the pastor*): You priests have a strange idea of Christian dignity.

DON COSTANTINO (*recovers his breath and his patience*): Why can't you try to be serious and reasonable? Reflect at least on this point: In most civilized countries, Christianity is now accepted by all classes of society. We can't go on meeting in catacombs, or in stables, the way you do.

FRA TOMMASO: Sometimes, yes, we do meet in stables. You know why? Certainly not because we love dirt, but because you prevent us from preaching in church. And since Christ was born in a stable, no priest should be allowed to speak of them with scorn, as you do.

FRA LUDOVICO: Ten years or so ago, even in our province in the Marches, there came the news that Fra Pietro del Morrone, before resigning as abbot of the order he had founded, sold the chalices and the other precious objects of his churches to distribute the proceeds among the poor. Truthfully, father, do you believe that, in so doing, he compromised his authority and lost his dignity? We were inspired by what he did and that was when we conceived the idea of coming to him in pilgrimage.

DON COSTANTINO (*to Fra Ludovico*): A person can criticize certain aspects of ecclesiastical usage and even act contrary to them, and yet remain a devoted son of the Church. Like Fra Pietro, in fact. Why don't you imitate his humility and his obedience? Instead you are filled with a spirit of rebellion and no longer have any respect for authority.

FRA LUDOVICO: We may have some differences of opinion with Fra Pietro. We will discuss them with him, fraternally. But how can you say that authority must always be obeyed? What if authority is in error?

FRA BERARDO (*furiously indignant*): It's scandalous for a Christian to place obedience above the truth.

DON COSTANTINO: Children cannot judge their father. And the authority of the Church—you know this as well as I—is based on power directly delegated by Christ.

FRA TOMMASO: Don't you think that there might be unfaithful delegates? When betrayal is obvious, must a man go on obeying? If, for example, the head of the Church preaches hatred and blesses arms—the opposite of what Christ taught—must Christians continue to obey him?

FRA LUDOVICO (*to Fra Tommaso*): Why speak hypothetically? Our words are clearer if we are more concrete and precise. First of all, who represents the authority of the Church at this moment? In the absence of a pope, the Sacred College of Cardinals, gathered in conclave. For more than two years, since the death of Nicholas IV, the cardinals have been meeting to name his successor, first in Rome, then in Rieti, and finally in Perugia, without results. Why can't they come to an agreement? Is some serious question of faith involved perhaps? No. As everyone is aware, the princes of the Church are divided, almost equally, into two hostile factions, the Colonna faction on one side, and the Orsini on the other. They aren't worried about the disastrous conditions of the Christian people, but only about their own family interests. Can a more revolting sacrilege be imagined?

DON COSTANTINO: This is an hour of confusion and decadence that saddens all of us.

FRA BERARDO: It isn't an isolated incident. After the death of Clement IV, too, the cardinals took a good nineteen months before electing Gregory X.

[*Don Costantino bows his head, his eyes on the ground, as if absent. But the friars' accusations are implacable.*]

FRA LUDOVICO: The cause of these obscene spectacles is one alone, and everyone knows it. It's because the cardinals belong to the great Roman families, landowners and money-lenders. Each of them is greedy to add to his ill-gotten riches, laying hands on the patrimony of the Church and the Papal States.

[*Don Costantino nods sadly, without raising his head.*]

FRA TOMMASO (*partly addressing Matteo and partly the audience*): It's no good trying to console ourselves with the thought that these cardinals are old men. It seems they actually reproduce themselves in the family.

FRA LUDOVICO: Of course. Just to give you some examples: Cardinal Latino Malabranca is the son of Pope Nicholas III's sister—an Orsini. And Giovanni Buccamazio was made cardinal by Honorius IV, his relative, and he has been clever enough to become the lord of eleven castles and cities . . .

[*Don Costantino remains in a state of apathy, but continues to nod his head slightly.*]

FRA BERARDO (*to Fra Ludovico*): What about the story that canon in Chieti told us of the Grand Penitentiary?

FRA LUDOVICO: It's connected with the election of the new pope. After the death of Nicholas IV, the cardinals decided that the powers of the Grand Penitentiary were also suspended and, along with them, those of the diocesan penitentiaries.

So for two years many tormented souls have been waiting for the election of a new pope, who will set the penitentiary system working again.

DON COSTANTINO (*recovers himself and stands, for a moment, to reinforce his words*): In spite of everything you have said and everything you might add; in spite of our sins, our mistakes, our betrayals . . . well, the Church, in the long run, cannot err, because she is protected by the promise and the intercession of Christ. And I'll say something further. The very fact that she still survives is a confirmation of her divine origin.

MATTEO (*shyly, after coughing to clear his throat*): Forgive me, a simple layman, if I dare speak up. I've heard it said that, after many clashes, even bloodshed, the Orsini and the Colonna families reached a compromise for the position of senator in Rome. Couldn't they do the same for the Holy See?

FRA LUDOVICO: God forbid. The solution for the seat in the Senate was, as they say, Solomonic; instead of one, they created two senators, a Colonna and an Orsini. Would you want to have two popes?

MATTEO: Oh, no, no.

DON COSTANTINO (*pulls himself together*): Your criticism is honest and just, but can't you realize that your behaviour only increases the disorder? The opposite of one error is often a more serious error.

FRA TOMMASO: The duty to disobey superiors who betray their trust is sacrosanct, it is the most Christian of duties. Conscience is above obedience.

DON COSTANTINO (*seems terrified*): Do you realize the consequences of what you are saying?

FRA LUDOVICO: How can you refuse a just principle out of fear of the consequences?

DON COSTANTINO: It seems to me disorder is the worst form of injustice.

MATTEO (*gets off the sawhorse, where he has remained during the whole discussion, and stands between pastor and friars*): All the time you've been exchanging arguments, I've been asking myself: how can we have come to this? After all, Saint Francis died only about sixty years ago. My grandfather saw him and heard him, and he loved to tell us how the saint came by here on his way back from Celano. He rode over the Caruso pass on a donkey, but when he went uphill and when he wasn't surrounded by a crowd, he preferred to go on foot. The whole population of Sulmona went out to meet him, and many walked all the way to Raiano. In all his humility and simplicity, the Poor Man of Assisi seemed Christ returned to the earth. Indeed, many believed he was Christ reincarnate. What's left now of all that immense fervour, of that teaching, so clear and so unmistakable? His relics are preserved, even some hair of his donkey's mane, but his words . . .

FRA LUDOVICO: His words were betrayed, even before he died, by the infamous Frate Elia, with the support of the pope and the bishops. The Franciscan concept of poverty, for them, represented a threat to their privileges and those of their families.

FRA CLEMENTINO (*as he continues his turns along the last step*):

> Poverty is having nought
> Poverty is wanting nought
> Poverty is having all
> In freedom's spirit, freely sought.

DON COSTANTINO: The Franciscan rule of 1223 contains more reasonable precepts. Why don't you follow them? (*Again the pastor seems to have put his foot into a hornets' nest. The friars surround him aggressively.*)

FRA LUDOVICO: Those precepts were put in against Saint Francis's will. Frate Leone's testimony leaves no doubt on that score. The Saint was mortally wounded by it.

FRA BERARDO (*vehemently*): The truth preached by Saint Francis is the truth of the Gospel, and no pope or council can change it; those popes who try to do so excommunicate themselves, and anyone who obeys such popes becomes their accomplice and damns his own soul.

FRA TOMMASO: Why should monks and priests be allowed what Christ didn't allow the apostles?

DON COSTANTINO (*forces himself to smile, to be conciliatory*): Human society has developed in an unforeseen way; you should realize that yourselves. You take the Gospel literally and continue to follow the teaching of Joachim of Fiore with its prophecies about the imminence of the Third age and the Kingdom of God. A noble prophecy, but . . . has it come about, after all?

FRA LUDOVICO (*bursts out laughing*): Pastor, it seems to me you're confusing the ages of the Spirit with the due-dates of lotteries and usurers' policies. Be a little more patient with our Heavenly Father.

FRA BERARDO: As far as that day and that hour are concerned— we have been told—nobody knows them, not even the angels in heaven, nor the Son . . . only the Father.

FRA TOMMASO: The hour will come, Christ said, like a thief in the night.

FRA CLEMENTINO (*same tone as before*):

> To be myself, not for myself,
> To live alone, not be alone:
> This is my task, my joy, my goal,
> Until my life is done.

DON COSTANTINO (*conciliatory*): In spite of your physical hardships and your persecutions, all things considered, you have the better part. You're fortunate, though, that there are few of you. What would happen if the majority of the people followed you?

FRA CLEMENTINO: What Fra Jacopone da Todi called "holy nihilism".

DON COSTANTINO: Anarchy?

FRA CLEMENTINO (*laughing*): Why not? It's a way of living together in charity, not by laws.

FRA LUDOVICO (*to the pastor*): I don't know whether you've ever meditated on the first book of Samuel, where it is written that the barren woman will bring forth more children than the fertile woman.

[*Suddenly from the left, the gendarme reappears.*]

GENDARME (*to the pastor*): I'm at your orders (*in a whisper*), my men are all ready, here in the vicinity.

DON COSTANTINO: Ready for what? There's no need. We've had an interesting conversation, I'd say, a very friendly talk.

GENDARME: Have you made a note of their names? The bailiff is expecting them. (*Murmurs something into the pastor's ear.*)

DON COSTANTINO: Those suspicions are unfounded. I'll speak with the bailiff.

GENDARME: I don't like to insist, but he's waiting for me to bring him the list of names. He says he's had specific warnings and must check.

DON COSTANTINO (*embarrassed*): That is not my duty; I'm a pastor.

GENDARME (*irritated*): But it was your people who made the request . . . I mean it came from the bishop.

DON COSTANTINO (*before going away, approaches Matteo and says to him in a low voice*): The bailiff has received an outrageous accusation against you and Concetta, you can't imagine. Let me know if anything comes of it.

[*The pastor and the gendarme go off, engaged in a heated discussion between themselves.*]

MATTEO (*to Fra Ludovico*): I'm afraid something will come of it, many things.

THE TWO-FOLD VOCATION OF FRA PIETRO ANGELERIO

Matteo and the friars gather together and are talking in whispers, when Fra Bartolomeo da Trasacco arrives unexpectedly. He is a monk from the Abbey of the Holy Spirit. He has a knapsack over his shoulder and the appearance of a strong, kindly old peasant. He wears the white habit and black hood of the Morronese monks.

MATTEO (*consoled by this arrival*): Welcome, Fra Bartolomeo, you're sorely needed.

FRA BARTOLOMEO (*affably*): Peace be with you all.

FRIARS: And with thy spirit.

FRA BARTOLOMEO (*gives Matteo the knapsack*): Our abbot sends you some bread and a few onions for your guests. (*To the friars.*) Where are you from?

FRA LUDOVICO: From Macerata.

FRA BERARDO: From Penne.

FRA TOMMASO: The two of us (*nods towards Fra Clementino*) are from Atri.

FRA BARTOLOMEO: Macerata, Penne, Atri are glorious places to be from, lands rich in Franciscan history; good, good. Fra Pietro was told of your arrival and naturally he wants to meet you. Among other things (*to Fra Ludovico, in a lower tone*) he is eager to have news of Pietro da Fossombrone.

FRA LUDOVICO: Is Fra Pietro's refuge far from here? Could someone take us to him at once?

FRA BARTOLOMEO: He isn't far away, but the path there is toilsome. Fra Pietro is concerned about the age and the health of some of you.

FRA TOMMASO (*smiling*): Unless I've been misinformed, he is older than we are.

FRA BARTOLOMEO: Yes, by many years, but he grew up in the mountains. The path that leads up to his hermitage is steep and in one or two places even dangerous. Some of those who want to visit him have to turn back when they are half way there. (*Smiles.*) Fra Pietro had his reasons for choosing that spot. But he is sorry for you and your friends, and he says that since you have already come so far he will meet you in the plain. Would you mind meeting him at the abbey?

MATTEO (*to give the friars time to overcome the embarrassment caused them by this invitation*): Why don't we sit down? (*To Fra Bartolomeo.*) These friends have just arrived after a long journey.

[*They form a circle, two of them sit on the first step of the stairs, the others on the ground.*]

FRA BARTOLOMEO: I wouldn't like my invitation to the abbey to be misunderstood. I thought you would all be safe there; neither the bishop nor the bailiff would dare bother you. But I know and respect your dislike of the big convents.

FRA LUDOVICO: I thank you for your sincerity. We can speak to each other openly, without discourtesy or reticence. If we've come this far, aware as we are of the differences of opinion between us, it's because we also have many points in common.

FRA BARTOLOMEO: We want to help you, but only in the way that pleases you. No more than that. Fra Pietro once explained to us that the differences between us, after all, are those that existed between Saint Benedict and Saint Francis.

FRA LUDOVICO: Unfortunately, it isn't easy to live up to their example. On hearing those names, Saint Benedict, Saint Francis, a man feels his knees bend. As a rule founders are eagles; their followers are more often like hens.

FRA BARTOLOMEO (*laughs long and heartily, to the delight of the others; then he abruptly turns sad*): Yes, it's true, in any large body there's always a tendency towards the chicken-coop. But I'd like to ask you if you think that simply by remaining outside it . . .

FRA LUDOVICO: Oh no, it's not enough. Even outside, in the open air, you can become tamed.

FRA CLEMENTINO: Like farmyard chickens, so to speak. (*To Fra Bartolomeo.*) Tell us about Fra Pietro, what he's like. Is he stern, is he sad? Does he joke?

[*Since Fra Bartolomeo remains silent, the others insist.*]

FRA BERARDO: When we meet him, we don't want to ask him useless questions . . . that's the only reason we want to know.

MATTEO: You may already know that Fra Bartolomeo was one of Fra Pietro's first companions in his hermit life, about fifty years ago, with Angelo di Caramanico, Berardo di Guardi-

agrele, Francesco d'Atri and a few others. Our mountain
seemed a beehive then, and Fra Pietro's little group, at that
time, was a tiny swarm which, every two or three years,
shifted from one place to another, avoiding the intrusion of
the curious and also of those who demanded benedictions
or even miracles.

[*Long pause, as they wait for Fra Bartolomeo to speak.*]

FRA BARTOLOMEO: It isn't meet to pronounce panegyrics for a
man who, thank God, is still living. What can I tell you?
Perhaps this is enough: all in all, he is truly a good
Christian.

FRA LUDOVICO: You're right. Idle praise doesn't interest us; we
want to know his way of thinking and acting. How does he
stand, now, with the congregation of the Morronese
monks, which he founded—if I'm not mistaken—forty
years ago?

FRA BERARDO: Is it true that he's broken away from them in the
meanwhile?

FRA BARTOLOMEO: No, that isn't correct. (*Long pause.*) There is
one thing that's important in understanding Fra Pietro. He
is a Christian who has had the grace of two vocations, and
both exceptionally strong, almost irresistible, I'd say: the
vocation of the hermit, and the vocation of the shepherd of
souls.

FRA LUDOVICO: Others have also had two vocations, and that can
be the cause of great sorrows. It's a fortune, I mean, that
can become a misfortune.

FRA BARTOLOMEO: As a hermit, when he was young, at the time I
met him—and I'm speaking of fifty years ago—Fra Pietro
was a simply marvellous man. You could hear him sing
the praises of the Creator in the most unlikely hours of the
night; you could see him play and talk with the wildest
animals, a fox, a snake, and other creatures of the mountain; you could watch him pray and you discovered what a
happy man he was, a man with his soul at peace. Mount
Palleno itself, where we had taken refuge in those early days,

seemed transfigured. The mountain was often bathed in a clear light I've never seen again, in any other place. A young man from Caramanico, who hadn't found himself a cave, built his cell at the top of an oak, to be near us, and that tree was always crowded with birds of every sort. But as the years passed, Fra Pietro's fame began to attract more and more of the faithful to his refuge. They were young people who asked to be guided, but not just with a sermon; they wanted to be led, day by day, working under his orders. How could he send them away? Shepherds came, too, and other poor men from whom he heard horrifying tales of the poverty, the injustice, the abuse, the wickedness of the nobles, and also of the sloth, the complicity, the corruption of the secular clergy. The day came when Fra Pietro could stand it no longer. He began to tell us we should be ashamed to flee from those laments, moving from one cave to another, hiding. He wasn't able to sing any more. The starry nights became hateful to him. Finally he decided to go down from the mountain and gather his friends together. Though no one could have predicted it, in his new task he showed extraordinary practical ability. It was obvious he had been born to lead other men. (*Pause.*) Forgive me. I've lapsed into the very panegyric I wanted to avoid. (*Motions that he has nothing further to say.*)

MATTEO: It's difficult for a good Christian to ignore the fate of his fellow-men. The older brother can't neglect his younger brothers. Christ went into the desert, but only for a while.

[*The friars are silent and look at Fra Ludovico, as if to suggest he is the most suited to reply. Since he is silent, Fra Bartolomeo adds something.*]

FRA BARTOLOMEO: According to Saint Matthew, Christ promised his disciples: where two or three are gathered in my name, there am I. He didn't say: when you are alone, or when you are far from the world.

FRA LUDOVICO: Perhaps he didn't mean to say, either: I'll be with you when you're in the midst of the crowd, when you are organized in a great assembly of people, with directors and assistant directors, and leaders of every sort.

FRA BERARDO: He said simply: when two or three of you are gathered together.

FRA BARTOLOMEO: You're right. Still it seems to me unchristian to scorn the flock. The majority of men are unable to follow your bold, free example. And yet, even the weakest creatures have a right to salvation. Christ died for them, too.

FRA LUDOVICO: Of course, Fra Bartolomeo, of course. But how is the flock to be saved? A large community is a dangerous, almost diabolical machine, even for those who are part of it. Experience shows us that a large community spontaneously kindles ambition for power, desire—never really sated— for success and triumphs. In the noble aim of advancing the community, constant compromises and adjustments are accepted. Does this happen because of the leaders' ambition or because of the flock's demands? I don't know, it may be that in most cases the two egoisms are united, and I'm willing to assume that the leader's intentions are good. In other words, it seems natural to me that, in the interest of the community, and to the greater glory of God, an abbot or a prior or a guardian might not want to arouse the hostility of the authorities, or of the rich, since he needs their help to establish new convents, build new churches, obtain new bequests, dispensations, privileges, winning them away from rival communities. As a community gradually becomes larger, it inevitably resembles the society that surrounds it. And then? What becomes of the salvation of the flock?

[*Fra Bartolomeo is silent; he looks at the ground. This encourages the other friars to take up the discussion, with no hostility towards him, however.*]

FRA BERARDO: It's sad, but there's no way out. If the land

belongs to the rich, where can you build a convent, unless you receive land from them? And if the rich donor, as often happens, is a tyrant, or corrupt, or an outright criminal, it becomes impossible to condemn him. I think this explains why Fra Pietro resigned as abbot of his order and went back to the mountain.

FRA TOMMASO: Joachim of Fiore resigned as head of his order, too. And so did Saint Francis. A large community demands compromises which an honest man—much less a saint—cannot accept.

FRA CLEMENTINO (*arguing against his companions*): Do you believe then, that it's all just a question of numbers? There were twelve apostles, the twelfth was a traitor. Is eleven the limit, perhaps?

FRA BARTOLOMEO: No, even among fewer than twelve, there can be a traitor. In Pilate's tribunal, the Master was denied by the first of the twelve, by the very one on whom he had decided to build his Church. I think fidelity isn't a question of numbers. Don't you believe that a man can sin even when he is alone?

FRA CLEMENTINO: No good Christian is ever completely alone. When he prays, he doesn't say: My Father. He says: Our Father.

[*As if by surprise, a curious character arrives and rapidly runs in a circle around the little group in conversation. The newcomer, who is nicknamed Cerbicca, looks like a rustic, with the manners and grimaces of a clown: agile, gay, and at the same time obsequious and familiar with all, even with the strangers.*]

CERBICCA: Oh, here are my lords and masters at last. Do you know how long I've been waiting for you?

MATTEO (*recognizes him and immediately tries to drive him away*): Cerbicca, there's nothing for you here. Leave us in peace.

CERBICCA: Unless I'm mistaken, these noble strangers don't belong to that monkery that preaches poverty in public and then swills and gorges in the convent. It was one of them, last year, preaching during Lent, who explained to us that Saint Francis considered money no better than dung and urged every good Christian to look on it in the same way. After the sermon I ran into the sacristy and, just to do the preacher a good turn, offered to carry away any kind of filth he had, in his pocket or in the cupboard of the convent. You know how he received my generous offer? He opened the door and, not saying a word, he kicked me out.

[*Laughter.*]

MATTEO: Cerbicca, now that you've managed to make us laugh, you can go.

CERBICCA: But first I want to inform these noble strangers that I'm theirs to command if they need a means of transportation. My rates are not afraid of competition.

FRA BARTOLOMEO (*laughing*): Have you bought yourself a carriage?

CERBICCA: No, but I now have at my disposal a splendid beast of burden.

MATTEO: How did you buy it?

CERBICCA (*imitating a preacher's voice*): He who looks after the birds in the air and the flowers of the field can come to the aid of a creature made in His own image.

FRA BARTOLOMEO: Are you perhaps speaking of a donkey? I saw him, following you, yesterday evening on the Pratola road?

CERBICCA: You saw him, my lord? You must have seen something else.

FRA BARTOLOMEO: Ah, really? He looked like a donkey, all the same.

CERBICCA: He looked like a donkey, and he was a donkey, my lord. But there was a little mistake. He is a female.

FRA BARTOLOMEO: Did you steal her?

CERBICCA: You're joking, my lord. Didn't you observe that the animal was following me of her own free will?

FRA BARTOLOMEO: I observed that she was following the sack of straw you had under your arm, undone in the back, and she managed to snap at it from time to time with her hungry jaws.

CERBICCA: My lord, surely you don't mean to reproach me for the little Christian charity I offered a poor, abandoned animal? As you saw me yesterday evening, I hope you also noticed that several times, with kindly words, I urged the creature to go home, to her family. "Go away," I said to her, "go away, people around here are suspicious; who knows what they might think of the two of us?" But it was all in vain. So I was suggesting therefore to these foreign gentlemen . . .

[*He breaks off abruptly.*
The gendarme, seen a short time before, reappears in the square.]

GENDARME (*to the peasant*): Cerbicca, what are you doing here?

CERBICCA: I was talking, more or less, or by and large, about religion with these old and glorious schoolmates of mine.

GENDARME: I didn't come here looking for you, Cerbicca, but now that I've found you, I have a little question to ask you. A peasant from Pratola reported the theft of his donkey to us this morning. Do you know anything about it?

CERBICCA: A donkey has been stolen? There's no limit to human wickedness these days. How could anyone separate a donkey from his loved ones?

GENDARME: Since you've been sentenced for theft on other occasions . . .

CERBICCA: Unjustly; these old friends can bear witness, am I right? Unjustly, always unjustly.

GENDARME: Clear out for the moment, anyway; I'll talk to you about this later. At present I have other things to do.

[*Cerbicca goes off. The friars stand up and gather around Fra Bartolomeo. Matteo shuts the door of his house and stands on the threshold, as if guarding it.*

GENDARME: I am to ask the foreigners not to go away. The bailiff will arrive to see them any moment. You, too, Matteo, and your daughter have some accounts to settle, so stay here and await his pleasure. As for you, Fra Bartolomeo, you may go.

FRA BARTOLOMEO: I prefer to stay with my friends.

GENDARME: I meant that you are not involved. Anyway, here comes the bailiff.

THE SECULAR ARM IS EMBARRASSED

The bailiff, who is charged with administering minor penal justice, has the appropriate uniform and manner, as well as a little pointed beard and high leather boots.

BAILIFF: Fra Bartolomeo, my respects. We've known each other for many years. How many? I couldn't say, but it doesn't matter. Your presence doesn't disturb me, but I must beg you not to interfere in the inquiry I'm forced to make concerning these individuals, whose identity, for that matter, is still to be ascertained. (*To the friars.*) Have you papers, documents, of any kind, ecclesiastical or civil, which can establish who you are?

FRA LUDOVICO (*takes a little wooden crucifix from his pocket and holds it under the nose of the bailiff, who steps back in disgust*): Do you know this? Do you consider it valid?

FRA BARTOLOMEO (*conciliatory, to the bailiff*): They are our friends. I can testify for them.

BAILIFF: It is precisely out of respect for you and for the pastor Don Costantino that I spoke so benevolently to them, and also to avoid the scandal of escorting them in chains to the seat of justice. You know, Fra Bartolomeo, how easily the local population becomes wrought up. I have therefore deigned to come here myself, in person. (*To the friars.*) Since you cannot produce any documents of any sort, please be so kind as to follow this gendarme to my office.

[*In reply, the friars sit down, scattered over the stairway.*]

GENDARME (*in the tone of a military order*): All right, let's go.

FRA LUDOVICO: It's impossible. We are very tired. We've already walked far enough.

BAILIFF (*restraining his anger*): My office is nearby. Now stand up and obey.

FRA LUDOVICO: Your office, I must inform you, is not a part of our plan. We haven't come all the way to Sulmona to visit offices. Such places, unfortunately, can be found everywhere.

BAILIFF: What are you afraid of, if you have clear consciences?

FRA CLEMENTINO (*though Fra Ludovico motions to him, in vain, to control himself*): If you would be good enough to explain to us what you mean by a clear conscience, magnificent sir, you would probably make an original contribution to the history of humour. Come, speak up, don't be shy.

BAILIFF: None of your insolence, young man. (*To the whole group of friars.*) For the last time, I order you to stand up and follow me and the gendarme.

FRA LUDOVICO: Forgive me, but, apart from any other consideration, have you ever seen two people imprison four?

BAILIFF: What do you mean? Are you defying me? Is this an insubordination?

FRA CLEMENTINO: No, don't be afraid. It's a simple, arithmetical equation. The law of numbers is the first of the profane laws.

GENDARME (*to the bailiff*): Shall I send for reinforcements?

FRA BARTOLOMEO (*with great satisfaction*): They're coming now.

A MAN OF GOD

Ahead of time, Fra Pietro arrives. He is wearing the white habit and black hood of the Morronese monks, like Fra Bartolomeo, but he is slightly older, tall, thin, erect and vigorous in his bearing despite his age. As soon as he glimpses the group of friars on the steps, he holds up his arm in greeting.

FRA PIETRO: Peace be with you, my brothers.

FRIARS (*spring to their feet, replying with festive gestures and voices*): Hurrah, hurrah.

FRA CLEMENTINO: Our soul doth magnify the Lord . . .

BAILIFF (*drawing the gendarme to one side*): This old nuisance would turn up now (*turning to Fra Pietro, he takes off his hat and makes a deep bow*).

FRA PIETRO (*to the bailiff, in a jesting tone*): What are you doing? You don't want to deprive me of my friends?

BAILIFF: You consider them companions of yours?

FRA PIETRO: Certainly, they are mine, and, if they accept me, I am theirs. Otherwise why would they have come from so far away to visit me?

BAILIFF: Still, they don't dress like the Morronese monks.

FRA PIETRO: Men may be sons of the same mother and yet dress differently.

BAILIFF: From the law's point of view . . .

FRA PIETRO: Forgive me, but what law are you speaking of? Civil law, or canon law? You shouldn't intervene in the Church's internal questions.

BAILIFF: Quite so. But do these distinctions still exist? I don't think so. Or, at least, they have lost some of their distinctness. Perhaps you haven't heard that our king, the glorious Charles II, spoke a few days ago in the conclave at Perugia. It's a great event, a historic event, as you will understand.

FRA LUDOVICO (*to his companions, with a grimace of disgust*): That's all we needed, a king in the conclave.

FRA PIETRO: Up at the hermitage, as you can imagine, news arrives late. I'm sure the king intervened to settle the discord, and anything that can contribute to peace within the Church makes me rejoice.

BAILIFF: As for them (*points with contempt at the friars*) I must make it clear that the denunciation against them came from the Papal States and was transmitted to us by the bishop.

FRA PIETRO: We are in the Kingdom of Naples here, not in the Papal States. As for the bishop, he has perhaps forgotten the ties that bind us Morronese monks to the Spiritual Franciscans. The Morronese order receives great moral benefits from them, even if the Spirituals are not a part of our order.

BAILIFF: You are of the opinion, if I understand you properly, that protecting these individuals is one of your rights? Well, for my report to the bishop and to the Grand Justiciary, I may tell you, that will be enough.

FRA PIETRO (*shifting from a severe tone to a benevolent and paternal attitude*): Yes, we have the right, but not only the right. You are a bailiff, but, first of all, you are, like the rest of us, something more important.

BAILIFF (*curious*): What's that? I'd be amused to know.

FRA PIETRO: You're a Christian, aren't you?

BAILIFF: Oh, yes, I was baptized. For that matter, we all are around here, as soon as we're born.

FRA PIETRO: Now it's true that we first become Christians through the grace of Baptism, but we remain true Christians only if we love one another. Jesus said this and, mind you, it wasn't simply a figure of speech.

BAILIFF: My position as bailiff, however . . .

FRA PIETRO: I must also add that we Christians have a special obligation towards these friars. It is in the interest of all Christianity that the teaching of Saint Francis be preserved in its purity, even if the situation of the Church, for the moment, is what it is, and for some people any reminder of the real Saint Francis may be cause for remorse. Bailiff, I mean that Christians like you and like me need to have friends who have gone farther than we have, and if we see them in danger, it's obvious that we must help them.

BAILIFF (*stunned*): I should help . . . them?

FRA PIETRO: And here, among these mountains, there is a great tradition, even older than the coming of Christ: the tradition of hospitality. For our most remote ancestors, bailiff, according to the natural law impressed upon their hearts, a guest was sacred. And this applies to these poor men who have come to visit us, on foot, from another province. To persecute them here, in our home, would be a horrible sacrilege. Forgive me if I seem to be teaching you a lesson. I have no doubt you feel these things more deeply than I do.

BAILIFF (*seems confused, he steps back until he bumps into the gendarme, to whom he mutters something which the others can't hear*): I give you my word of honour, this man is mad.

FRA PIETRO (*to the friars*): If you are not entirely pleased with my way of speaking, please contradict me. We are not lawyers, our strength doesn't lie in any display of words, but in our sincerity.

FRA LUDOVICO (*to Fra Pietro, in a moved voice*): We thank you for every word you have uttered. I don't say this just for the expediency of the moment.

[*The bailiff makes a great gesture of renunciation. He takes Fra Pietro aside, however, to confide something in him. Cerbicca, who has just come back into the square, slips up behind him.*]

BAILIFF: You may know more than I do about this, Fra Pietro, but it's my duty to inform you that among these individuals, I mean among these so-called Spiritual friars, there are men of every stripe, and even some outright rogues.

FRA PIETRO: That may be, but I see no sign of it.

BAILIFF: Do you know that one member of their sect, before the ecclesiastical tribunal of Macerata, even confessed that he had fornicated with the wife of the devil?

FRA PIETRO: He confessed? But a man of the law like yourself, bailiff, knows better than I what an expert judge can make a chained defendant say. And if that defendant told the truth, we must deduce from his confession that the devil is properly married. So he isn't the total rebel they say he is.

CERBICCA (*stepping between the two*): Ah, is that why he's always shown with horns? The poor devil's married. (*The bailiff doesn't immediately recognize Cerbicca, but is nevertheless annoyed by his interference. The man goes on insistently.*)

There's one thing I don't understand, however. How can it be a sin to do the devil a bad turn! (*The bailiff tries to go off, but Cerbicca follows him.*) One other question: the lucky friar, I mean the accused . . . did he give the address of the prodigal lady, did he furnish details? Is she young? Plump?

BAILIFF: Leave me alone. That's all I know.

CERBICCA: You've forgotten to tell us the essential part. Did the friar have to pay, or did the good lady . . .

BAILIFF (*finally recognizes him*): Ah, it's you, is it, Cerbicca? How dare you take such liberties? (*He grabs him by the arm and shows him to Fra Pietro, who had moved away.*) This man even dared steal in church. Yes, he took the poor box, in the presence of the most Holy Sacrament exposed on the altar.

CERBICCA (*protests indignantly*): That's not true, it's slander. The poor box was behind the column of the holy-water font, and from the altar He absolutely couldn't see me. Besides, on the box it was written "For the poor", and inside there was almost nothing.

[*The gendarme tries to kick Cerbicca, but the man eludes him and runs off. The friars, with Fra Bartolomeo and Fra Pietro, move meanwhile to the upper steps of the church to talk among themselves. Matteo remains on guard at the door of his house.*]

THE PARABLE OF THE COOKED BEANS

GENDARME (*to the bailiff*): Are we to go back to the office empty-handed?

BAILIFF: You don't expect me to cross swords with Fra Pietro, do you? You know that even the Grand Justiciary of the king protects that madman.

GENDARME: Still we could take out a little revenge on the weaver. Have you forgotten the baron's report?

BAILIFF: A meagre satisfaction, but better than nothing. (*To Matteo, arrogantly.*) Call your daughter. I have a summons for the two of you.

[*Matteo opens the door and calls Concetta, who seems, however, reluctant to come out of the house.*]

CONCETTA (*whispering*): Father, I think I recognize the wolf I dreamed of last night.

MATTEO: Don't be afraid, child, Fra Pietro is still here.

[*Father and daughter, side by side, stand in the doorway, his hand holding hers.*]

BAILIFF (*to Concetta*): There is a serious complaint that concerns you and also involves your father, as the head of the family. Have you ever set foot in the baron's house? I mean in years past.

CONCETTA (*after thinking it over*): A few times, several years ago, I went there to take some skeins of wool to his daughter, who had asked me for them.

BAILIFF: Were the skeins of wool paid for?

CONCETTA: Yes, the normal price.

BAILIFF: You received nothing beyond that?

CONCETTA: Beyond the price? I don't think so.

BAILIFF: Didn't you receive, each time, a bowl of beans?

CONCETTA: Yes, now I remember. Three or four times. It was close to supper time, and the servant used to take me to the kitchen and give me a bowl of beans.

BAILIFF: Were the beans a part of the price of the wool?

CONCETTA: No, they weren't owed to me.

BAILIFF: Well, the baron, being a great lord, naturally doesn't trouble himself to recall such trifles, but the maidservant who took you into the kitchen remembered this a few days ago. She recalled those bowls of beans because of the recent scandal you caused in our parish, fomenting the Daughters of Mary against the baron and the other lords. So the maid reported her recollection to the steward of the baron's household, and to punish you for your ingratitude, he has presented a petition to the court, asking to be repaid for the beans which you did not deserve.

MATTEO: They were a gift. Obviously, a gift and not a loan. And besides, after all, a few bowls of beans . . .

BAILIFF (*ignoring Matteo's remark, takes a sheet of paper from his pocket. The group of friars interrupt their conversation to follow the scene*): The steward has therefore calculated precisely the amount he can claim from you, bearing in mind the harvest that the given number of beans would have produced if sown in good soil, like the fields of the baron, and if, year by year, each harvest was regularly sown again, up to and including the present year. In a spirit of equity, beyond any question of private interest, we, of the law, had the calculations examined by an expert who found them exact. So it is my duty to give you a copy of the calculations by which your debt to the baron's household has been determined.

MATTEO (*examines the paper, aghast*): Thirty sacks of beans? Where could I find them?

BAILIFF: We give you a week's time. Aren't we generous? Of course, in addition you must pay the legal expenses.

[*In the meanwhile Fra Pietro has come down the steps and approached the bailiff, with the others behind him.*]

FRA PIETRO (*to Matteo and Concetta, smiling*): Don't worry.

BAILIFF (*visibly irritated by Fra Pietro's presence*): Fra Pietro, I'm sorry, but canon law has nothing to do with this case, and it's not a question of foreigners, but of people in this city. Nobody can deny, it seems to me, the right of the baron's steward to demand restitution of what belongs to the household.

FRA PIETRO: Since the beans were a gift, that right could easily be denied, but in this case it's unnecessary. If I follow you then, a maid of the baron's offered Concetta, on various occasions, a bowl of beans? Is that right? So it's a matter of calculating what those beans would have produced in all these years.

BAILIFF (*reassured*): Quite so; the case is clear, a matter of a precise calculation. Matteo, if he chooses, can call his own expert.

FRA PIETRO: Matteo, will you entrust this task to me? Thank you. You know, as a boy, in the country around Isernia, I also grew up among beans and peas, so to speak, but in this case no great experience is required. The calculation is easy. Now, it's a question of knowing what remains, after a few days or a few years, of one or more bowls of cooked beans, whether they are eaten and digested or whether, for one reason or another, they are thrown in a furrow and buried. (*To the bailiff.*) With all due respect to yourself and the baron's household, it seems to me the answer is obvious: a bit of manure remains. You say that the baron's steward absolutely insists on its restitution?

BAILIFF (*white with rage*): If that's what it is, I'm sure he doesn't insist. In any case, thank you for the offer.

[*The bailiff and the gendarme go off to one side. Fra Pietro and the others, incuding Matteo, go off in the opposite direction, while Concetta remains confused, dazed, at the door of the house. Fra Clementino turns towards her and abruptly comes back.*]

FRA CLEMENTINO (*in an affectionate, subdued voice*): The poor are not always forgotten to the very end, so unhappy people go on hoping.

[*Darkness falls.*]

II

The Hermitage of Sant'Onofrio, July, 1294

THE "MIRACULOUS" CONCLUSION OF AN IMPOTENT CONCLAVE

The hermitage known as the "Eremo di Sant'Onofrio", halfway up Mount Morrone, in a narrow clearing created among rocky cliffs. The path leading to it is very steep, and it ends at the left of the stage. On the right, closed off by some loose planks which serve as a door, is the cell where Fra Pietro lives. A young Morronese monk, violent in his movements and his appearance, is on guard at the end of the path. From time to time he makes an angry gesture, to repulse would-be visitors to the hermitage, warning them to come no farther. On some large stones, set against the rocky wall, two other friars are seated: Fra Ludovico, the Spiritual Franciscan we have already encountered, and the Morronese monk, Fra Angelo da Caramanico, one of Fra Pietro's first companions. His fellow-monk, Fra Bartolomeo da Trasacco, whom we also know, is near the entrance to the cell, waiting to be called. The rustic door has an opening which lets in some light and air and allows one to peer inside. It is just after dawn.

YOUNG MORRONESE (*springs to his feet, enraged at somebody disobeying his order to go back. He admonishes him in a very loud voice*): No, no, scoundrel, rogue. No, I say.

FRA BARTOLOMEO (*alarmed, to his young fellow-monk*): Don't shout. I beg you not to shout (*and, with gestures, he explains —or rather, reminds—the young man that his shouts disturb the man meditating or praying in his cell*).

YOUNG MORRONESE (*lowering his voice*): May I throw stones then?

FRA BARTOLOMEO: Yes, but don't use your slingshot, however. And don't aim at anybody.

[*Fra Ludovico is sitting in silence, staring at the ground, lost in thought. From time to time, a brief gesture escapes him, as if he were arguing with himself.*]

FRA ANGELO (*solicitously*): What is it, Fra Ludovico?

FRA LUDOVICO: Forgive me, Fra Angelo. I'm still racked with the same doubt. Frankly, I can't believe it.

FRA ANGELO (*surprised*): You can't believe that our Fra Pietro has been elected pope?

FRA LUDOVICO: No, that's not what I mean. The election by now seems beyond any doubt. Down in Sulmona, I saw the prelates who came from Perugia with the message, and by pure chance I also witnessed the arrival of the King of Naples with his courtiers. What I can't swallow is the story of how the conclave arrived at the election. Let's be reasonable about it. How is it possible that, after twenty-seven months of talk and unseemly quarrels, one afternoon, the cardinals—all of them, we're told, without exception—suddenly agreed on this miraculous choice?

FRA ANGELO: Don't you believe in miracles?

FRA LUDOVICO: Yes, I can believe in them when they involve innocent shepherd-girls, and even then with all due prudence. But the conclave is made up of cardinals, who are anything but simple men, anything but innocent, anything but selfless. They are members of the aristocracy, appointed to the Sacred College not for their virtues but through the power of their families. Now for a good twenty-seven months the representatives of the Orsini, the Colonna, the Caetani families had been unshakeable, in a furious struggle to grasp the papacy for themselves, and then abruptly, those cynical, stubborn old men—deaf to the real needs of Christianity...

FRA ANGELO (*interrupts him*): But Fra Ludovico, cardinals—or, if you prefer, *even* cardinals—are God's creatures, subject to His will.

FRA LUDOVICO: However, Christ never showed the slightest interest in them. Fra Angelo, you know as well as I do that Our Lord didn't even look them in the face and preferred to deal with fishermen and artisans.

FRA ANGELO (*laughing*): My dear Fra Ludovico, what are you saying? In Christ's time there weren't any cardinals.

FRA LUDOVICO: They went by another name. They were called High Priests or something of the sort, but as a class they've always existed. Well, Our Lord never troubled himself to convert the members of the Sanhedrin or to work miracles with them. At least this is what the Gospel tells us.

FRA ANGELO: The Spirit blows where and when it pleases. You, Fra Ludovico, belong to the so-called Spiritual Franciscans, so how can you refuse to believe in the infinite power and freedom of the Holy Spirit?

FRA LUDOVICO (*after a moment's reflection*): Then, to your way of thinking, Fra Angelo, a new Pentecost took place at the conclave in Perugia? Was there a clear, violent, irresistible descent of the Holy Spirit on the cardinals, who were struck with confusion? Is this what you mean?

FRA ANGELO (*seriously embarrassed*): How can I answer you? Your question is terrible, Fra Ludovico, it's beyond my poor mind. (*After a pause, he goes on.*) But this much is certain: the session of the conclave in Perugia at which our Fra Pietro was elected didn't proceed in any usual way. Just think: after the voting all the cardinals wept.

FRA LUDOVICO (*shaken, but still incredulous*): They wept? The cardinals?

FRA ANGELO: This detail was confirmed by each of the people from Perugia.

[*As the morning proceeds, the light becomes brighter, more rosy, and a merry chirping of birds is heard all around the hermitage.*]

FRA ANGELO (*to Fra Bartolomeo, pointing at the cell*): Is he resting?

FRA BARTOLOMEO: No, he's praying.

FRA ANGELO: Has he eaten anything?

FRA BARTOLOMEO (*rather than raise his voice he comes over to the other two*): He hasn't touched any food for three days. Every now and then he drinks some water.

FRA ANGELO (*in a benevolent tone, nodding towards the friar*): Our Fra Ludovico is still upset.

FRA LUDOVICO: Please forgive me, dear friends; I would gladly share in your rejoicing. When I succeed in driving doubts from my mind, they return to me in the form of visions. And so, a little while ago, as I was praying, I watched the sun rise on the Maiella, and in that glowing sphere I thought I saw the severed head of the Baptist. (*He covers his eyes with his hands, as if to drive away the vision he believes tragic.*)

FRA BARTOLOMEO (*with a cry of joy*): But this vision of yours, Fra Ludovico, was a good sign. What could be more consoling than the Baptist, triumphant in the sun, while the star is over our Maiella?

[*Fra Ludovico smiles.*]

FRA ANGELO: Yes, the hour has come that was promised to our fathers, Fra Ludovico. The dove has prevailed over the eagle. You, too, should open your heart to hope.

FRA BARTOLOMEO (*with ingenuous fervour*): When God so desires, nothing can resist His divine will. He exalts the humble, and casts down the proud. See how nature herself seems transfigured. This valley has never been so beautiful and so radiant. Have you ever seen such clear air?

[*The muffled echo of festive bells and fireworks begins to rise from the valley below. It is the hour when the pope-elect is expected in the city, for the formation of the procession that is to lead him to l'Aquila, where his coronation will take place in the church of Santa Maria di Collemaggio. From time to time, snatches are heard of the* Te Deum *and other lauds chanted by choruses of women, children, mountaineers, some of whom have climbed up the lower slopes of the mountain.*]

YOUNG MORRONESE (*to Fra Bartolomeo, with a large stone in his hand*): I think I see a Monsignor coming up. Shall I throw it at him?

FRA BARTOLOMEO: Frighten him, but don't hit him.

YOUNG MORRONESE (*towards the valley, with gestures of repulsion, threatening stones*): Hey there, go back. Back.

FRA BARTOLOMEO (*from the edge of the path, also observing the man who is approaching*): He's a messenger of the Episcopal Curia. We can't prevent him from coming up.

[*After a moment a young prelate appears, sweating and panting. He is too breathless to speak.*]

FRA ANGELO: Peace be with thee. Sit down, catch your breath.

EPISCOPAL MESSENGER: Why all this delay? Where is His Holiness?

FRA BARTOLOMEO (*nodding towards the cell*): He's praying.

EPISCOPAL MESSENGER: Could you announce me?

FRA BARTOLOMEO: While he's praying? Impossible.

EPISCOPAL MESSENGER (*timidly*): His doubts haven't come back again, have they?

FRA BARTOLOMEO: No, we can reassure you on that score. He's made up his mind now.

EPISCOPAL MESSENGER: God be praised. You know, I was in the Curia with the prelates from Perugia when one of your monks came in. He told us that when Fra Pietro first heard the news of his election, he ran away and was nowhere to be found. There was a moment of panic. Nobody knew what to suggest if the holy man were to persist in his refusal. The history of the Church has no precedents for such a situation.

FRA LUDOVICO: Obviously, all large organizations operate according to precedents. Therefore the rule of Saint Francis, having no precedent . . .

FRA ANGELO (*hastens to interrupt, to keep the conversation on a courteous level*): Fra Pietro's acceptance wasn't an easy matter.

FRA BARTOLOMEO: And his pontificate won't be easy.

EPISCOPAL MESSENGER: The whole diocese is in a state of unparalleled excitement.

FRA BARTOLOMEO: The old people say that something similar happened sixty years ago when Saint Francis passed through the district.

EPISCOPAL MESSENGER: In Sulmona now even the Ghibelline families are rejoicing; in fact, they are especially pleased.

You mustn't forget that almost half the men of Sulmona are still in exile, because they sided with the Swabians.

FRA BARTOLOMEO: They know that Fra Pietro has promised a general pardon and the return of the exiles.

EPISCOPAL MESSENGER (*seized with impatience again*): Forgive me, but do you think we have much longer to wait?

FRA BARTOLOMEO: We have no way of knowing.

EPISCOPAL MESSENGER: I wouldn't like to seem importunate, but I was sent up here to press him. The official procession has gathered in the cathedral and they are waiting for His Holiness. The hour was set by general agreement, and it's already past.

FRA LUDOVICO: They aren't waiting on the road, after all. In the cathedral those who like can pray. It wouldn't be a waste of time, I should think.

EPISCOPAL MESSENGER: Naturally, of course, yes indeed. But the delegation of the conclave, as you may know, is composed of the Archbishop of Lyons, and by the bishops of Orvieto and Patti. Then, quite unexpectedly, just a little while ago Cardinal Pietro Colonna arrived.

FRA LUDOVICO: Pietro Colonna? The one who repudiated his wife and put her in a convent? Ha, ha, the ceremony will have to be revised a bit, I imagine. What role will you give Pietro Colonna?

YOUNG MORRONESE (*to Fra Bartolomeo, seizing a large stone*): A gentleman is coming up with a plume in his hat and a little sword at his waist. Can I throw at him?

EPISCOPAL MESSENGER (*after having observed him*): God forbid, young man. He's a messenger of the king.

[*A little later the gentleman appears, also somewhat wearied by the difficult climb, though still strong enough to display his annoyance immediately.*]

ROYAL MESSENGER: What are you waiting for? Don't you know you're terribly late? His Majesty Charles II and his son, His Highness Charles Martel, are all ready. To say nothing, of course, of the ecclesiastical delegation. Where is the pope-elect?

FRA BARTOLOMEO (*pointing to the cell*): He's praying. Please, don't raise your voice.

ROYAL MESSENGER: Can't you call him?

FRA BARTOLOMEO: Impossible.

ROYAL MESSENGER: As far as we're concerned, everything is ready, you understand? Everything, down to the last detail. Finally, a military scout has been sent along the road from here to l'Aquila, with the order to confiscate a hundred fatted kine.

FRA BARTOLOMEO: Didn't you know Fra Pietro eats no meat? A single lamb would have been too much for him.

ROYAL MESSENGER: If he doesn't eat meat, those in the papal party will.

FRA BARTOLOMEO: To tell the truth, we don't eat meat either.

ROYAL MESSENGER: Well, *we* do. (*Impatient.*) Can you tell me how long his prayers usually last?

FRA ANGELO: There's no foreseeing.

ROYAL MESSENGER: I've told you once and I repeat that His Majesty the King . . .

FRA ANGELO: Our respect towards His Majesty is beyond doubt.

FRA LUDOVICO: On the other hand, our Heavenly Father also is worthy of some respect, don't you think? And if Fra Pietro were talking with Him at the moment . . .

ROYAL MESSENGER (*curious*): Ah, you mean the Heavenly Father might be there at this moment, in that cave?

FRA LUDOVICO: Would that surprise you? Do you think He has a fixed residence in the sky, above the clouds?

ROYAL MESSENGER: I don't know, I'm not an expert in religion, you can't know everything. But, while we're on the subject, I'd like to ask you, the friends of the new pope, for some confidential information. It's a question I've heard asked by a number of people at court these days, and nobody was able to give an answer. The question is this: does he (*nodding towards Fra Pietro*) really believe?

THE TEMPTATION OF POWER

While the monks and the episcopal messenger are struck dumb by this unexpected question and exchange embarrassed glances, the door of the cell opens and Fra Pietro appears. He is wearing the usual Morronese habit. He seems thinner, and is shy and meek as usual.

FRA PIETRO: Peace be with you, my brothers.

MONKS: And with thy spirit.

ROYAL MESSENGER (*stepping forward with determination and making a deep bow*): I have been charged by His Majesty King Charles to place myself at Your Holiness's disposal for any requirement. I beg Your Holiness not to spurn my services. At the foot of this path I have already prepared, for Your Holiness's journey to l'Aquila, a magnificent, docile white horse, all decked in red, with an expert groom.

FRA PIETRO: I thank you. I must tell you, however, that my favourite mount, when the distance doesn't allow me to go on foot, is a donkey. (*The royal messenger seems about to insist, but Fra Pietro doesn't allow him to.*) Naturally, I have the greatest esteem for the horse, but I have my reasons for setting the donkey before him. Mind you, I don't mean to establish a rule, or to teach others a lesson. But, for myself, I feel that if I began to prefer a horse to the donkey, fine silk clothing to rough cloth, a richly-set table to a plain humble board, I would start thinking and feeling like those who ride horses, live in grand drawing-rooms and eat banquets. Personally, I don't think religious authority has any need of luxury to inspire respect. In any event, even in my new station, I don't intend to abandon the way of living of the poor, to whom I belong.

[*The royal messenger is aghast and hides his confusion in another deep bow of apparent agreement. Then turning to his monks, Fra Pietro recognizes among them the Spiritual friar whose presence he had been unaware of. He goes to him at once, embraces him, and draws him aside, neglecting the others.*

FRA PIETRO: I know that in these past few days you've had doubts about the decision I had to make, the same doubts I had. I thank you. It wasn't an easy choice, as you can imagine. I have spent hours and hours in spiritual communion with the abbot Joachim, with Saint Benedict, with Saint Francis, but even from them I received divergent inspirations. If I accept, I said to myself, won't I be sinning in my presumption? I'm a humble, ordinary Christian; how can I dare become the vicar of Our Lord among men? Then this doubt was followed by another, its exact opposite. And if, rather than commit the sin of presumption, I were committing the sin of cowardice, lacking faith in the Holy Spirit and his assistance? How many centuries would have to go by before another opportunity like this presented itself? The case, precisely, of a humble ordinary Christian named to that throne which for too long a time has been reserved for the offspring of the great princely houses? If I refuse, I said to myself, how can we go on complaining that the Holy See allows itself to be drawn into conflicts among princes and even blesses fratricidal arms instead of being a centre of peace and fraternity? How can we lament that the teaching of Saint Francis, recent as it is, has been wilfully misconstrued and his most faithful followers denounced to the ecclesiastical courts? But as soon as I leaned towards acceptance and I reflected on my imminent obligations, I felt my spirits fail again. I asked myself: where will I find the learning, the wisdom, the experience that I lack? Whom can I trust in the Curia of Rome?

FRA LUDOVICO (*moved*): My father, you know well what is written: God tempts no one beyond his strength. I can say more. Perhaps you don't realize it, because these past days you've been shut up in a cave, but the expectation among good Christians is immense. Don't you believe that this, too, is a source of strength? I heard with my own ears a peasant weeping with joy and repeating: "Finally we'll have a pope who believes in God."

FRA PIETRO: But it's precisely this excessive expectation that makes my head swim. (*The royal messenger and the episcopal messenger begin to clear their throats discreetly.*) Forgive me, Fra Ludovico, these gentlemen are reminding me I'm late. Just one more thing, please: send word at once to Pietro da Fossombrone and some of the other men in his confidence that I expect them at l'Aquila with you. I have absolute need of all of you. (*To the others.*) Forgive me. We can go now. (*He starts off; at the top of the path he stops for a moment.*) I'll take the name of Celestine. I shall be Celestine V.

[END OF PART ONE]

III

Naples. October, 1294

A great, half-dark room in the Castelnuovo, near the port, in Naples, the temporary residence of Celestine V. As the situation requires, the room serves as papal antechamber and as the private audience chamber. On the right side of the room there is a door which is usually closed, since it is reserved for the king and his messengers. Next to it is a little door on which "Clausura" is written, to indicate the cell which the pope has desired for himself. On the same wall is painted the coat of arms he has selected: a rampant lion. In the rear wall a balcony overlooks the Piazza delle Corregge. At left a large door leads to the other state rooms.

Fra Bartolomeo da Trasacco and Fra Angelo da Caramanico, whom the pope has chosen as personal assistants, are busy arranging the scant furniture of the room: an armchair, some straight chairs, a rug, a table with a crucifix on it, a candelabrum, and some papers.

FRA BARTOLOMEO: Again this morning, complaints from Rome. Why is Pope Celestine staying in Naples, they say. The apostolic seat is in Rome. Does he prefer to act as chaplain to the King of Naples?

FRA ANGELO: Yesterday evening the Archbishop of Benevento, contradicting Cardinal Caetani, decreed *ubi papa ibi Roma*. Still, it's clear we can't stay long here in Naples.

FRA BARTOLOMEO: I don't know how our Celestine will manage to overcome his repugnance of the Roman Curia and the duties of the ruler of the Papal States, which he'll have to carry out in Rome.

FRA ANGELO: He isn't entirely wrong. They are two great misfortunes.

FRA BARTOLOMEO: Do you remember when we used to add to the litanies of the saints: "from the Roman Curia *libera nos Domine*"? But, frankly, Naples also has its drawbacks.

FRA ANGELO: The worst thing about Naples is the Neapolitans. And then our Celestine can't bear this heat. His health is really in an alarming state. Have you noticed how much trouble he has breathing?

FRA BARTOLOMEO: After sixty years of life in the mountains, it isn't easy to become used to a seaside city. And this bay seems the chapter-house of the sirocco.

[*The sound of a bell is heard. Fra Angelo draws the curtains of the balcony aside and illuminates the room.*]

FRA ANGELO: It's time for the weekly hearing of petitions. (*From the balcony he observes the square.*) The crowd grows bigger every week.

FRA BARTOLOMEO: See if people in the crowd are still bringing hens, cheeses, hams for the Monsignors of the petitions office.

FRA ANGELO (*leans over the balcony and looks more closely*): I can't see any. After our Celestine's furious outburst, I don't believe the Monsignors . . .

FRA BARTOLOMEO: They'll give the petitioners their home addresses. Or else they'll accept ready money. They're not the sort to retreat in the face of certain difficulties.

THE MORRONESE DISAPPOINT POPE CELESTINE

Preceded by two acolytes with lighted candles, the pope appears in the door at left, returning from the chapel where he has celebrated the Mass. He is wearing a simple white alb with a little wooden crucifix around his neck. Fra Bartolomeo and Fra Angelo receive him with a deep bow.

CELESTINE V (*to the acolytes*): You may go.

[*The pope answers his monks' greeting with a gesture and a smile, then goes towards the table.*]

CELESTINE V (*seeing a parchment*): News from Fra Jacopone da Todi. Was he here? You should have told me.

FRA ANGELO: That message was left us by Pietro da Fossombrone . . .

CELESTINE V: He's called Angelo Clareno now, don't forget that. And his friend Pietro da Macerata is called Liberato. The new congregation of the poor hermits is in good hands. (*Sits down and reads.*) "What will you do, Pier da Morrone? You to the fray now have come . . ." (*He resumes his examination of the other documents; soon he makes a brusque gesture of impatience and addresses the two monks.*) Have you read these other requests from our people in Sulmona and Atri? Have you seen how far the greed of our priors and abbots can go? (*The pope is deeply disheartened, he sets his forearms on the table and rests his head on them; afterwards he resumes, in a dejected voice.*) They exaggerate. I've already given generous privileges to the congregation. I've enriched their monasteries with churches, lands, forests, grazing meadows, taking them from the bishops and from other religious orders. I've given much; or, to tell the truth, I've given too much. Well, have you read their latest requests? As if I weren't informed on the turn life in our monasteries is taking. They live like new rich, and they're not yet sated. The newly-rich rarely consider themselves satisfied. Do they think mine is the pontificate of milk and honey? Do they think I'm a Camorra leader?

FRA ANGELO and FRA BARTOLOMEO (*trying to intervene*): Father . . .

CELESTINE V: What distinguishes our monasteries now from the Conventual Franciscans? As far as I can see, nothing. Why did we criticize the Conventuals then? Why did we mock the nepotism of the popes of the past? Was it only envy? (*An attack of asthma prevents him from going on, but little by little he recovers himself.*) Since I've been here, I haven't lacked mortifications; but, more or less, I expected them and I accepted them without bitterness, indeed, with gratitude, as occasions for exercising humility. But the most painful wounds are those I receive from my own family. I am ashamed before God, because responsibility for the misdeeds of a family falls on the father first of all. What a disappointment. I hadn't expected this. In fact, I expected the contrary. I said to myself: I know my weaknesses, I am old, I haven't sufficient learning, I'm inexperienced in the things of this world, and I can't ask God to do everything. But in the hard trials that await me, at least in the essential ones, I won't be alone, I'll have a spiritual family behind me, the sons I've educated . . .

FRA ANGELO and FRA BARTOLOMEO (*as before*): Father . . .

CELESTINE V: In other words, I thought the congregation could be of help to me in the struggle to restore the health of the Church, in that return to the Christian way of life, to evangelical poverty and simplicity, which I don't have to explain to you. That was the reason why, rashly and stupidly, yes, stupidly, I concerned myself with strengthening our convents as quickly as possible, lavishing privileges and gifts on them. I forgot that a fat horse can no longer run.

FRA BARTOLOMEO: Father, the last word hasn't yet been spoken.

CELESTINE V: I should have acted in the opposite way, expropriate them, throw them out on the road, to the four winds, subject them to severe trials.

FRA ANGELO: Would you like to leave us the task of answering those letters? Will you allow Fra Bartolomeo and me to make a visit to our chief monasteries in the next few days?

CELESTINE V: We'll talk about it later. Now I must rest. (*He goes towards his cell.*)

FRA ANGELO: In the afternoon, just after Vespers, there's the audience of the Neapolitan preachers named for Advent.

CELESTINE V (*embarrassed*): This afternoon? No, today I really don't feel up to it. The Neapolitan preachers are famous talkers, and I'm not ready to face them. Please, postpone the audience until next week.

[*The pope disappears into his cell, and the stage grows dark.*]

A SIMPLE MAN AMONG RHETORICIANS AND COURTIERS

After a brief pause the lights come up, and some changes are visible on the stage: Fra Angelo is seated at the table, where he is putting some parchment scrolls in order. A short distance from the door, facing it, there is a prie-dieu with an armchair. On the shelf of the prie-dieu there is a crucifix and a candlestick with a candle in it. From the drawing room next door a murmuring is heard, typical of an assembly before it comes to order. From the general noise isolated remarks emerge: "Where have they assigned you to preach this year?", "I don't understand you; are you hoarse?", "Oh, my dear Don Cecè, what? Still a free man?", "I'm delighted, or rather, I'm encouraged", "My word of honour, I swear"; and repeated hushings: "Don't raise your voice", "Quiet, you'll disturb the Holy Father". In the doorway, around the prie-dieu a little group of priests and monks forms, in view of the audience; they exchange personal impressions of the new pontiff, keeping an eye on Fra Angelo, however, who might be listening.

VOICES: "Have you met him yet? Is it true that he only speaks Abruzzese dialect?"

"Have you seen the little cloistered room? Does he sleep in there? On the floor?"

"That's where the Holy Father talks with the Holy Spirit?"

"The door next to it is reserved for the king."

"Is it true that the new pope never touches meat? Not even chicken?"

"Just vegetables. Preferably raw." (*Laughter.*)

"He must have his special weaknesses, perhaps in secret."

"So it seems. Radishes." (*Laughter.*)

"Good Heavens."

"Drink? Of course, he drinks."

"Yes, milk."

"Just milk? Like infants?"

"Not like infants. He doesn't suck woman's milk, but sheep's or goat's." (*Laughter.*)

"How about the miracles? Does he still work some from time to time?"

"Have you heard that amusing story about him at Lyons, in France? Listen. When he went to Lyons, at the time of the council, to obtain recognition of the Morronese order from Gregory X, he happened one day into a room full of people, and nobody paid any attention to him. So he threw his cowl into the air and it hung there, from a ray of sunshine, like a hook . . ."

"Marvellous. Was the miracle put on record?"

"Let's ask him to do it again today, for us."

[*From the little cloistered room the sound of a bell is heard.*]

FRA ANGELO (*stands and announces in a loud voice*): The Holy Father.

[*Suddenly there is silence. The men who were chatting by the prie-dieu hasten back to their places. The little door of the cell opens and Celestine V appears in his usual white alb with the wooden cross around his neck. Accompanied by Don Angelo, he heads for the prie-dieu and for a moment observes the men present in the great hall. Fra Angelo lights the candle and remains with the pope, at a respectful distance.*)

CELESTINE V (*in a louder voice*): My children, peace be with you.

PREACHERS' VOICES: And with thy spirit.

CELESTINE V: Let us pray.

[*The pope kneels and prays in silence, making the Sign of the Cross at the end. As soon as he has risen, a prelate appears in the doorway with a long scroll in his hand. He makes a brief genuflection before the pope.*

CELESTINE V: What do you wish?

PRELATE: With Your Holiness's permission, I would like to read, in the name of all the preachers here present, an address of homage to Your Holiness.

CELESTINE V (*benevolently*): Thank you, there's no need. Please, go back to your seat.

[*Murmuring, shifting of chairs and coughing in the hall. The pope speaks very slowly, raising his voice.*]

CELESTINE V: Beloved children, even those of you who as yet don't know me personally are already aware that you mustn't expect from me a lesson in holy oratory. I know such an art exists, with its rules and models; but I confess humbly to you, I have never studied it, whereas I have heard that some of you are most expert in the art and are even famous. Bear in mind, too, that for many years I have led a hermit's life, a life where one speaks very little. So I will talk to you informally, as a father to his children, and I ask your pardon in advance if I am boring, as a father often is when he is speaking to children more educated than himself. In any case, I will limit myself to only two admonitions. First of all, I must say to you: when you preach, if it is possible, try to be simple. Ah, I know it's not easy to speak with simplicity. To succeed, obviously, we have to be simple within ourselves, and true simplicity is a very difficult achievement. A Christian's whole existence, you might say, has precisely this aim: to become simple. (*Murmuring from the other room.*) But if some of you have not yet won the grace of simplicity make an effort to obtain it at least in your way of expressing yourselves. Therefore, I beg you paternally to use words that everybody understands in your sermons. The word of God is addressed to every creature and especially to the humble. To those who find speaking simply most difficult, I can suggest this expedient. Each of you, I imagine, has dealings with some uncultivated person, a labourer perhaps, who knows barely his own job and nothing else. Well then, before giving your sermon in public, repeat it to him, privately, and eliminate every word he doesn't understand. (*Murmuring, coughs.*) My second admonition is more important. There is a proverb that says: mind what the priest says but not what he does. This proverb was no doubt invented by some preacher for his own convenience. (*Laughter.*) But, I assure you, Christians think and judge differently, and in my opinion they are absolutely right. They pay more heed to what priests or monks do than to what they say. Christianity, in fact, is not a way of speaking, but a way of living. And no one can decently preach Christianity to others if he doesn't himself live as a Christian. This is, therefore, my paternal suggestion: my dear preachers, do you want to be believed? Try to be good Christians, do good and do it with all your hearts. Don't do it out of cleverness, or for profit, or to be popular, or to advance your career. Do good gratuitously and tell nobody about it. Especially since God sees you in any case and will reward you, if not in this world, in the next. But even if God were paying no attention to you or were to find your virtue entirely natural—it takes great presumption to insist God concern Himself with each one of us—do good still, for it is a fine thing, a beautiful thing to do. Frankly, what is more beautiful? (*Murmuring.*) I believe I've said what I wanted, I thank you for having listened to me, and I bless you.

[*The pope raises his arm and slowly gives his blessing. As he goes away, followed by Fra Angelo, the murmuring in the next hall grows louder until the darkness extinguishes it.*]

THE DECEITS OF A VENAL CURIA

After a brief pause, the stage is illuminated again. The prie-dieu is there no longer, and the room has its usual appearance. The pope is seated at the table, his head resting against the high back of his armchair. He is motionless, his eyes half-closed. Along with a great weariness, we can sense a painful suffering in him. The taper in the candlestick is lighted. The pope seems unaware of the arrival, from the adjoining great hall, of the prelate acting as his private secretary, with a voluminous bundle of scrolls and parchments to sign.

*The secretary is a plump, ceremonious character, servile and sly.
Celestine's natural modesty and his inexperience have often
encouraged the secretary to assume the attitude of adviser or even
of preceptor. He speaks therefore as if to a child or a simpleton,
accompanying his words with superfluous gestures of explanation.*

SECRETARY (*with a brief hint of a genuflection, setting the bureau-
cratic bundle on the table*): Your Holiness . . .

[*The pope looks at him, giving no signs of wanting to listen
to him.*]

SECRETARY: Your Holiness . . . Are you listening to me?
CELESTINE V: What do you want?
SECRETARY: It's your secretary, I've come for the usual formality
of the signatures. Today again there are some urgent
matters, as well as, of course, the usual outstanding
business which we are trying to deal with, a bit each week.
(*The secretary takes the goose-quill on the table, dips it into
the little inkwell, and hands it to the pope, imitating the act
of signing.*)
CELESTINE V: Let me see. I want to examine one document at a
time. I have my reasons for doing this.

[*The pope's tone of voice is quite new, almost icy, very
different from his customary, paternal, kindly tone. The
secretary is astounded by it.*]

CELESTINE V (*examines the first parchment the secretary hands to
him*): I don't see any documentation for this, or the
summary in the vulgar tongue.
SECRETARY: Latin, Your Holiness, is the official language of the
Church . . .
CELESTINE V: If you have other such pieces of information, you
may spare me them. I had decided that each document
given me in Latin was to be accompanied by a summary in
Italian, for my personal use, to make the reading easier.
(*Pause. He seems uncertain whether merely to repeat the
order, or to take the trouble of explaining it again; finally*

his patience prevails.) I've explained before that my
knowledge of Latin is limited to the words of the Mass and
of the Holy Scriptures. Now, in these parchments, secular
and legal questions are often dealt with, and I'm not used
to them. (*He sets the documents aside, at a corner of the
table.*)

SECRETARY (*not hiding his surprise, almost his shock, since this is
the first time the pope has refused to sign*): Isn't Your
Holiness going to sign it? The letter was drawn up by His
Eminence . . .

CELESTINE V (*with irony*): You think perhaps that the pope
should sign without knowing what the letter is about?

SECRETARY (*dumbfounded, hesitating to give him the following
parchment*): This one is accompanied by the documentation.
There, you see?

CELESTINE V (*reads carefully*): Mainz? Where is that exactly?
Abroad, I imagine.

SECRETARY: When I was a student, it was beyond the Alps.

CELESTINE V: We may presume it has remained there.

SECRETARY: Mainz was the city of that famous Archbishop who
took part in a siege of Ancona, bringing a great number of
concubines with him.

CELESTINE V: I see that you are an expert in sacred history.
(*Pause.*) Who is this baron?

SECRETARY: He is asking for the annulment of the excommunication inflicted on him by your august predecessor. (*Hands
the pope the pen to sign.*)

CELESTINE V: I know nothing about this gentleman. (*Puts the
parchment on top of the other, already set aside.*)

SECRETARY: Isn't Your Holiness going to sign this one either?

CELESTINE V (*pays no attention to him*): What's next?

SECRETARY (*pale and confused, hands the pope another parchment*):
Here again, as you can see for yourself, a lengthy documentation is furnished. It's an old litigation between a
Benedictine abbot of Einsiedeln, in Switzerland, and the
abbess of the convent of Zurich. I've read all the documents,
so I can report on them to Your Holiness. The suit concerns

an annual rent in wax and honey which the abbot claims
and the abbess insists is now extinct. You know, Holy
Father, how women are . . .

CELESTINE V: I don't know and I'm not interested.

SECRETARY: Two years ago the abbot and the abbess decided to
put the question up to the arbitration of Your Holiness.
Since then they have, on several occasions, requested a
decision.

CELESTINE V (*reads hastily*): If I understand rightly, the abbot
insists that the abbess is lying, while the abbess makes the
same accusation against him. How can I judge? I don't
know them. I would have to go up there, listen to them, take
information; but can I make this journey? No. And even if
I could, I'm not sure I would reach an unerring opinion,
not at all sure.

SECRETARY: The abbot has the cardinal on his side . . .

CELESTINE V: If I'm the one who has to make the decision, I
would prefer to know who has the truth on his side. (*He sets
the parchment on the others.*)

SECRETARY: Allow me humbly to remind you that they have
appealed to the decision of Your Holiness and they've
been waiting for two years.

CELESTINE V: I'm not in a position to pronounce judgment conscientiously. In this condition no honest man would
demand a decision; this rule goes for the pope also, doesn't
it?

SECRETARY (*profoundly upset, presents the next document with
some difficulty*): This is a local provision, an administrative
matter, which already has the approval of His Majesty the
King.

CELESTINE V (*reads carefully in an audible voice; as he goes on, his
voice changes considerably*): "Apostolic Decree which sets
aside for the construction of a shrine in honour of the Immaculate Virgin the proceeds from the surtax imposed by
the Royal Government on those frequenting the brothels
of the zone of the harbour of Naples . . ." What is this
filth? Whose idea was it?

SECRETARY: If you are referring to the plans for the church in honour of the Immaculate Virgin, I can assure you that the architect . . .

CELESTINE V (*in a loud, indignant voice*): No, I'm referring to the surtax on houses of ill-fame in favour of the Virgin Mary.

SECRETARY: I understand Your Holiness's irritation, and naturally I share it. Perish the thought! I am and will always remain on Your Holiness's side. But simply for your information I might add that those places are very ancient institutions and, it seems, irreplaceable. Indeed, there are those who claim that it is the world's oldest profession. Even the ancient Egyptians, I repeat what I've heard, I wasn't there myself . . .

CELESTINE V: Leave the ancient Egyptians out of this. Here it's a question of Neapolitans today.

SECRETARY: Well, Holy Father, in the opinion of doctors, it seems that those places cannot be done without. Especially in ports and in garrison cities, wherever many sturdy men are living apart from their wives. The doctors say . . .

CELESTINE V: They say it can't be done without? That's not true. In any case, the Immaculate Virgin can very well do without a church constructed with stinking funds, can't she? Now tell me who conceived this shameful project.

SECRETARY (*frightened, he returns to his role as subaltern*): I will enquire, Holy Father, I promise you. Of all things. Personally I know nothing about it. Besides, who am I? A humble shifter of documents, the least important of men. My only merit, if I can call it that, is my absolute devotion to Your Holiness . . . I might also say . . .

CELESTINE V: Go on.

SECRETARY: No, I've already said too much.

CELESTINE V: You were about to add something further. You said: I might also say . . . and then you were silent.

SECRETARY: Didn't I add anything?

CELESTINE V: No.

SECRETARY: Ah, this is what I was about to say. No later than last week, you signed a decree for Civitavecchia similar to this one, with the only difference that the proceeds were assigned not to the Immaculate Virgin but to her mother, Saint Anne.

CELESTINE V: How can that be? Why didn't you warn me at the moment when I was signing?

SECRETARY: The filial awe I feel towards Your Holiness . . .

CELESTINE V (*stands up, gripped by irrepressible disgust*): My God, my God, what filth, what abjection, what wickedness . . . Why didn't You leave me in the mountains, among my poor people? . . . I never imagined I would have to face such base deceit here, here, at the summit of Your Church. (*He turns menacingly to the secretary, who steps back, alarmed.*) I have already learned of several frauds perpetrated through signatures I made without any suspicion. But this last trap goes beyond every limit. (*Exhausted by his emotion, he sits down again and covers his face with his hands. After a long silence, the pope addresses the secretary again.*) Hurry to the legal office and ask, in my name, that the ignominious order for Civitavecchia be revoked.

[*The secretary hastily gathers up the various documents scattered over the table; a few scrolls elude him and fall to the floor. He bends to pick them up. Finally he bows before the pope with a deeper genuflection than usual and heads for the door. But the pope calls him back.*]

CELESTINE V: One moment . . . (*His voice is heart-broken, but already calm.*) Please forgive me for having spoken just now in wrath . . . Wrath is a sin and I repent . . . I maintain, however, the order I have given.

[*The stage grows dark.*]

COMMON SENSE PILLORIED FOR ITS INEFFICACY

When the light returns, we see two young clerks, under the supervision of the secretary, busily carrying into the pope's study parch-

ment scrolls, dossiers, and documents, arranging them on the table, on chairs, and on stools pressed into service for this use.

SECRETARY: Hurry up. We have to finish before His Holiness comes back from the royal chapel.

[*The clerks seem to be amusing themselves; they try to balance the papers on their heads or on one shoulder. Coming from the adjacent hall one behind the other, before setting down their burdens, they make turns around the chairs and the table, in a kind of ballet.*]

SECRETARY (*gruffly*): Don't act like fools. Be serious.

[*The clerks immediately assume the gestures of a funeral ceremony.*]

SECRETARY: Don't put the documents down at random. Arrange them by date, in separate groups.

FIRST CLERK (*observes some dossiers*): This one's been waiting for nine years. This one for seven.

SECOND CLERK: This one is fourteen years old; it dates from 1280. I'm surprised the mice haven't eaten it.

SECRETARY: They've sent them from Rome to us. The mills of the Lord grind slow. The Church doesn't count the years, but the centuries.

FIRST CLERK: The people concerned with these papers may be dead by now.

SECRETARY: That doesn't matter. The pope's decrees are valid in the next world. Have you forgotten the promise? "Whatsoever ye shall bind on earth shall be bound in heaven, and whatsoever ye shall loose on earth shall be loosed in heaven."

FIRST CLERK (*to the secretary, almost with envy*): Do you see the Holy Father every day? What good fortune for you.

SECRETARY: What a great responsibility, you should say.

SECOND CLERK (*fervently*): The present pope is a true saint.

SECRETARY: How can you tell? He doesn't wear a halo around his head, after all.

SECOND CLERK (*same tone*): Oh, you can see it in everything about him, in his gaze, his voice, the grace in every gesture he makes.

FIRST CLERK (*with intense affection*): You're right. That's the way I imagine the apostles; that's how I imagine, for example, Saint Peter: strong, rough, good, generous, loyal, perhaps even ingenuous, but with the ingenuousness of the saints.

SECRETARY: Don't waste time chattering. You must hurry. We're late.

FIRST CLERK: Are we to bring the whole archive here? There isn't room.

SECRETARY: Not the whole archive, silly, just the part I showed you, the papers waiting to be signed. His Holiness has decided to examine them one by one; he wants to form his own opinion on each.

SECOND CLERK: He won't have time left even to pray.

SECRETARY: I see a boy with common sense can understand things that elude a saint. Saints, my boys, are all right on altars, after their death; but while they're alive, they mean nothing but trouble.

[*The two clerks look at each other, surprised by this irreverent gibe at the pope, while the sound of a bell calls the secretary into the adjacent room.*]

SECOND CLERK: In this palace mocking the pope is becoming a parlour game. You know they call him the Maiella bear? They make me so angry I can't tell you.

FIRST CLERK: They repeat the most stupid stories about him, or else they make them up. The other day, at the house of my uncle, the canon, jokes about the new pope were the whole evening's entertainment. Mind you, there were ladies present, too. I wept almost all night.

SECOND CLERK: Yes, the jokes and stories are almost always base. You know the one about the finger-bowl? I heard somebody tell it this morning, as I was serving the refreshments, between sessions of the Commission on the Sacraments. Well, at the end of every meal, if you can call "meals" the scanty food the Holy Father nourishes himself with, they put before him a cup of tepid water for him to wash his fingers. Not knowing the custom, he drank it. After the first few times, the servant respectfully warned him of his mistake. At which the pope asked if the water was clean. "Of course," he was told. "If that's so," the pope said, "I must say that, at the end of the meal, I rather enjoy a sip of warm water." And he went on drinking it . . . You should have heard the Monsignors of the Commission laugh this morning.

[*The secretary reappears at the door of the study, followed immediately by Fra Angelo. The monk is very much surprised at discovering the huge mass of scrolls and papers that cover the furnishings of the papal study.*]

FRA ANGELO (*to the secretary*): Who ordered you to transform His Holiness's study into a warehouse?

SECRETARY: His Holiness himself.

FRA ANGELO: This seems strange to me; there must be a misunderstanding.

SECRETARY: He ordered me to show him all the papers waiting for his august signature.

FRA ANGELO: All at once? Or, perhaps, one by one, as he examines them?

SECRETARY: He already has one with him, on which he has been reflecting for three days without coming to a conclusion. Do you know that there are some important ecclesiastical courts which are unable to function because they lack papal ratification?

FRA ANGELO: Good news at last. Is it really true that they aren't functioning?

SECRETARY (*who doesn't perceive Fra Angelo's irony*): In short, I thought it was opportune for His Holiness to have an idea of the quantity of matters that are unsettled, some sent us from Rome, some new, and more coming in every day.

FRA ANGELO: Couldn't you make a list of them? Or else invite His Holiness for a moment or two into the offices of the

Chancellery? (*The secretary remains silent and, in keeping with his character, passes from bravado to fear.*) Were you being witty? Did you want, even you, to make a laughing-stock of the Maiella bear?

[*The secretary gesticulates, unable to utter a word. As he takes from his pocket a handkerchief to mop the sweat on his brow, a kid's horn falls to the floor. Fra Angelo hastens to pick it up.*]

FRA ANGELO: What's this? If I'm not being indiscreet, what use is it to you?

SECRETARY: Against the evil eye. All of us here carry something of the sort.

FRA ANGELO: You believe in it?

SECRETARY: I certainly do. Besides the evil eye is mentioned even in our creed. Haven't you ever noticed that? It says: *Credo in unum Deum factorem coeli et terrae visibilium omnium et invisibilium* . . . The Latin is easy: the *invisibilium omnium* obviously includes the evil eye.

FRA ANGELO (*hands the horn back to him*): Is this also prescribed in some liturgical act of ours?

SECRETARY: No. But it's recommended by our Neapolitan tradition, which is more ancient than Christianity.

[*Fra Angelo and the two clerks look at one another, amazed. The room grows dark.*]

THE PATER NOSTER CAUGHT IN THE MACHINERY OF ALIENATION

When the light returns, the study has resumed its normal appearance. Celestine V is seated in an armchair in the middle of the room, with an empty armchair beside him. There is a little package on the desk.

FRA ANGELO (*announcing from the doorway*): His Eminence Cardinal Benedetto Caetani.

[*The pope goes towards the cardinal, who greets him with a deep bow. As they take their places in the chairs, Fra Angelo withdraws and shuts the door after himself.*]

CELESTINE V: I thank you for coming to my aid. Your advice has always been of great help to me, even if I haven't always been able to follow it.

CARD. CAETANI: It is I who am grateful for the benevolence you have shown me . . . (*Breaks off and sniffs something unpleasant in the air.*)

CELESTINE V: Is something upsetting you?

CARD. CAETANI: Forgive me, Your Holiness, but what is this smell? In Naples they can't keep even the pope's residence clean.

CELESTINE V (*after looking around in embarrassment, discovers the source of the smell which is disturbing the cardinal; it comes from the package on his table*): Ah, it's the sheep cheese which arrived for me just now from Pescasseroli. There's a shepherd there who sends it to me regularly, because he's afraid the cheese in Naples might be poisoned. Here's an authentic story, to add to the others, more or less invented, that are already going around about me.

CARD. CAETANI: In every court there are fools who don't know how to fill their idle days. But I can assure you, Your Holiness, that here there are also serious people who look upon you with the veneration you deserve and regard your pontificate with absolute respect.

CELESTINE V: If you had come yesterday, you would have found this room transformed into a storehouse of parchments and codices of every sort.

CARD. CAETANI: I was told about that. Unfortunately, thanks to the long conclave, you've found an excessive pile of outstanding questions.

CELESTINE V: It grows every day, since I refuse to sign acts without full knowledge of their contents. It isn't easy for me, I assure you. On the other hand, I no longer feel like delegating sensitive assignments to people I don't know or resolving on the spot complicated suits when I have no idea of their origins or the litigants.

CARD. CAETANI: It's a difficult art and even the most expert make mistakes. Anyway you were right to rid yourself of that wicked secretary. As soon as you have one you can trust . . .

CELESTINE V: From now on I will not sign even the slightest scrap of parchment unless I know what it's about and unless I'm convinced the decision suggested to me is good. It was a serious error on my part to bring into this office, among outsiders and matters unfamiliar to me, the same trust I felt towards my monks. But I don't feel entirely without guilt in the excesses of my secretary.

CARD. CAETANI: From whom did you receive that fine character?

CELESTINE V: From a person above all suspicion, Giovanni di Castrocoeli, archbishop of Benevento and my vice-chancellor, whom you also know well.

CARD. CAETANI: Eh, eh, eh, you consider him above all suspicion? If that's the case, I'm sorry to have to announce further disappointments for you. His colleagues in the Curia have coined a motto for the archbishop of Benevento. While the rest of us believe in Father, Son and Holy Ghost, he believes in Father, Son, and Holy Most.

CELESTINE V: Perhaps you are unaware that sayings of the sort, perhaps less witty, also circulate concerning you. Am I to believe them?

CARD. CAETANI: Why not? But I defy anyone to prove that the events to which that gossip refers have in any way reduced my independence. But we can discuss that later. Now as far as the rascally tricks of the secretary are concerned, it is urgent for you to find a prompt solution, if possible without attracting the attention of the civil authorities.

CELESTINE V: Some of his knavery was discovered by the police themselves and it's beyond being remedied in silence. Such as the collecting of girls, some of them even minors, in the provinces of the Abruzzo, for the houses of ill-fame in the province of Naples. Do you know that this wicked traffic was disguised as a series of pilgrimages under the patronage of the Holy See? To crown his contempt, he called these false pilgrims "the Generous Celestines".

CARD. CAETANI: He and his delinquent associates, one would say, do not lack imagination.

CELESTINE V: But let us come to our own affairs now. What do you think of my plan to entrust all ordinary administration to a commission of three cardinals? Of course, they would assume public responsibility for their actions.

CARD. CAETANI: I'm sorry to say this to you, but I find it impossible. It would be like having three popes instead of one, or like giving three husbands to one wife. I know you've spoken of it also with other cardinals. If I'm not misinformed, all of them have opposed the idea.

CELESTINE V: Of course, it's convenient for all of you to have me as a scapegoat.

CARD. CAETANI: In this case at least, Your Holiness, the motive is more elevated. The reform you suggest would be contrary to our whole establishment. The structure of the Church is monarchical and could not be otherwise. One spirit, one body, one faith, one God, one vicar. And then, have you considered the composition of this presumed triarchy? It's probable that, in the distributive justice you have pursued in our regard, you would nominate an Orsini, a Colonna, a Caetani, or at least men we trust. Do you believe such a committee would act rapidly and in harmony? Can't you foresee it would call upon you to arbitrate any question of some importance?

CELESTINE V (*with a gesture of resignation*): If that's so, then I can only pray the Lord to give me patience. I'll go ahead by myself, as best I can, which is to say: badly. Do me one favour, however, and do not complain about the slowness of my secretariat. I cannot, I assure you, I cannot sign acts of which I am not sufficiently informed or convinced. If I study over a single case for a week, accuse me, if you like, of weakness of intellect. I can do nothing about that. My conscience, I repeat, doesn't allow me to make more rapid decisions.

CARD. CAETANI: I think I understand where the obstacle is. No, it isn't a question of intellect in the least. You believe it is obligatory—correct me if I'm mistaken—to follow in your office of Supreme Pontiff the same rule of simplicity that guided you in your previous duties. But your situation now is entirely different. No great political or military or religious organization can be governed like a family or like a small community. There's an enormous difference. Every great organization, if it is to function regularly, needs a certain number of pretences, without which it would lapse into chaos.

CELESTINE V: Must even the pope pretend then?

CARD. CAETANI: Could things be otherwise? It's not a matter of outright falsehood, but of conventions. You know, I suppose, that all state functionaries above a certain rank are royal nominations. That nomination guarantees each of them the necessary prestige, although the majority are quite unknown to the king. Similarly their sentences and decrees are pronounced in the name of the king, and therefore are accepted by his subjects as acts above discussion, sacrosanct. *A fortiori* this must apply to the Church, which is a vaster society, supranational, founded on divine revelation.

CELESTINE V: Isn't it a terrible thing that the Church of Christ is now organized like a State?

CARD. CAETANI: The State itself often apes the Church. What can you expect? Adversaries always resemble each other in the end, and the technique of command is more or less the same.

CELESTINE V: You'll probably pity me, when I tell you that, even in questions like this, I still go no farther than the Pater Noster and the Gospel. In the parables of the Gospel, you know as well as I, relations between men are always personal and direct. There is always the father with his sons or his servants; the owner of the vineyard with the workers; the shepherd with his sheep and his lambs; and so on. There are never indirect, anonymous relations, or pretences, or, as you would say, conventions. So you must forgive me if I cannot conceive Christian relations that are not personal relations. I mean to say: relations between souls, not things.

CARD. CAETANI: From the Gospel times to today—need I remind you?—society has grown, and so has the Church.

CELESTINE V: Yes, you're right, there are forces that drive men to become more and more alien to one another. But isn't it our Christian duty, in every new situation, to preserve the possibility for men to stay together, to understand one another, to love one another? Suppose a diocese becomes too large; nobody can prevent us, I should think, from subdividing it into two or three parts, so that personal relations, between pastor and faithful, will not suffer?

CARD. CAETANI: Why not? On the parochial or diocesan level I can agree with you. But the Church, as a whole, is a power now, indeed, the highest of powers, and she must behave as such. You can't govern with the Pater Noster.

CELESTINE V: Is this a limitation on my part? Probably it is, but I don't know what I can do about it. How can you reproach a poor man for continuing to behave, when he's a bishop or a pope, according to the rules of respect and benevolence he followed in his original environment? You might just as well have left him where he was. What does he have, if he gives up those very qualities that won him respect and the election?

CARD. CAETANI: No one demands such a sacrifice of you. But, in accepting the pontificate, you also knew, Your Holiness, that you were entering a much wider sphere, and that between you and Christianity a different relationship would be established from the one between yourself and the Morronese monks.

CELESTINE V: Christianity is very vast, yes, but still it's made up of souls, not of things. I can't treat Christians like objects, like stones, like chairs or tools, or even like subjects . . . I agree this attitude is inconvenient as far as rapidity and command are concerned, but it seems to me that here, too, there must be a difference between Christians and pagans. For Christians the supreme value lies in our consciences; so they merit the greatest respect. If I'm given the case of an ordinary person and I feel his salvation or his ruin may depend on my decision, how can I proceed in haste? It doesn't matter that he is unknown to me: he's a creature, a soul. It would be my duty to go and see him, converse with him, try to know him . . .

CARD. CAETANI: It's strange, truly strange. I never imagined a man like you could exist, absolutely unsusceptible to the sense of power.

CELESTINE V: That is a temptation that I, too, have known. But, with God's help, I believe I've overcome it.

CARD. CAETANI: It worries me very much. This creates a serious difficulty which, even in the near future, can have disastrous consequences for the Church. With your permission, Your Holiness, we must meet again as soon as possible and go into this matter thoroughly, with absolute frankness.

[*Darkness.*]

THE CONFLICTS ARE EXACERBATED

As soon as the light returns, the action is resumed in the pope's study, still slightly dark. Fra Bartolomeo and Fra Angelo are busy shifting chairs and arranging some parchments in order.

FRA BARTOLOMEO: His greatest weakness, it seems to me, is that he doesn't know how to give orders. Those who obey him become fewer all the time, and he lets the rest go.

FRA ANGELO: Once it wasn't like this. You remember how he made us toe the line at the abbey in Sulmona?

FRA BARTOLOMEO: The abbey was his family. When he raised

his voice, he was like a father scolding his children. I mean, he doesn't know how to give orders to strangers.

FRA ANGELO: When he first came here, he trusted everybody, it was easy to deceive him. Now he's suspicious of everybody. He's too much alone. We're of no help to him.

FRA BARTOLOMEO: We're like fish out of water here ourselves.

FRA ANGELO: Yesterday evening I talked with him about it. We're no use to you, I said to him.

FRA BARTOLOMEO: And what did he say?

FRA ANGELO: He looked at me with his eyes full of tears. Don't you understand, he answered, that without the two of you, I would already have gone away?

FRA BARTOLOMEO: He would already have gone away? Is that really what he said? Doesn't he realize, poor man, that by now he's condemned for life and there's no escaping from the papacy?

FRA ANGELO: You must have noticed that he's resumed his penitences. I have the impression that, for some time now, he's spent the nights lying on the floor. In the morning I see his pallet unrumpled.

FRA BARTOLOMEO: What makes him suffer most are his constant clashes with the king. In a strange way, he trusted the king more than the cardinals.

FRA ANGELO: Once he explained that to me. The king, he said, doesn't meddle with religion, whereas the cardinals . . .

FRA BARTOLOMEO: Do you believe the king was really sincere in supporting our Celestine's election?

FRA ANGELO: Why not? But, obviously, he was sincere in the manner of a king, I mean he had to make his calculations. Now that the sums haven't worked out, he's disappointed, naturally.

FRA BARTOLOMEO: This morning his military adjutant is coming for another audience. I took the liberty of suggesting to the pope that he refuse to receive the man, in view of his arrogance. So much the better, the pope answered, with arrogant men conversation is much more clear.

FRA ANGELO: He says that, but it makes him suffer.

[*The first clerk arrives with some documents which he hands to Fra Angelo.*]

FRA ANGELO (*to the clerk*): Your eyes are red. Are you ill?

FIRST CLERK: They're going to send me away from here. I wouldn't mind, except it means I won't see the Holy Father any more.

FRA ANGELO: Have you done something wrong?

FIRST CLERK: This morning, while I was serving an orange juice to some Monsignors in a Commission, the pitcher fell on the floor and broke.

FRA BARTOLOMEO: A moment's carelessness. That could happen to anyone. Are they going to send you away just for that?

FIRST CLERK: It wasn't carelessness. I threw it to the floor myself.

FRA BARTOLOMEO and FRA ANGELO: Why? What came over you?

FIRST CLERK: I did it to keep from smashing the pitcher over the head of someone who at that moment was saying bad things about His Holiness. (*Turns his back on the two monks to hide his tears.*)

FRA ANGELO (*laughing*): Come, come, this isn't the first time a Monsignor has made fun of the pope.

FIRST CLERK: He wasn't making fun of him; on the contrary, he was saying that the pope is putting the Church in grave danger.

FRA BARTOLOMEO: Who was it? Who was talking like that?

FIRST CLERK (*hesitates before answering*): I'm sorry, I can't tell you. I can't be an informer.

FRA BARTOLOMEO (*smiles at him*): You're right.

THE REFUSAL TO BLESS THE WAR

The sound of a bell announces the arrival of Celestine V. Fra Angelo and the clerk exit hastily. The pope sits in the armchair behind the table, while Fra Bartolomeo lights the taper in the candlestick and hands him the papers brought by the clerk.

CELESTINE V: The king's adjutant hasn't come yet?

FRA BARTOLOMEO: Not yet (*hands the pope the bundle of papers just brought in by the clerk*). There's an urgent request from the bishop of the Marsi for a privilege to be granted to the new church of Santa Maria della Vittoria at Scurcola Marsicana.

CELESTINE V: Santa Maria della Vittoria? For what victory is the Mother of Christ being honoured?

FRA BARTOLOMEO: They are certainly referring to Charles of Anjou's victory over Conradin of Swabia. You remember, a few years ago, there was that big battle of the French against the Swabians, around our parts, between Scurcola and Tagliacozzo.

CELESTINE V: Did Christ's Mother take part in the battle? Was she seen on the side of the French?

FRA BARTOLOMEO: Are you joking? But the French had been called in by the pope.

CELESTINE V: Not, surely, by the Mother of Christ. (*Angrily pushes away the parchment which was ready to be signed.*)

FRA BARTOLOMEO: Here is the king's adjutant.

[*The door at right, next to the cell's door, is flung open, and the king's adjutant appears. He stiffens in a military salute.*]

CELESTINE V: Come in and be seated.

[*The adjutant takes a seat beside the table. Fra Bartolomeo goes out.*]

ADJUTANT: I thank Your Holiness for granting me this audience. I was afraid I had left an unpleasant memory, after my brusque manner of expressing myself the last time.

CELESTINE V: On the contrary. I prefer the frank, plain speech of soldiers to the complicated talk of jurists and theologians.

ADJUTANT: I'll try not to abuse your patience. I'll begin with a message that means a great deal to me. His Majesty the King is deeply grieved at noticing a considerable change in Your Holiness's attitude towards him.

CELESTINE V: My affection for His Majesty hasn't changed, you can assure him of that. Since I have known him personally, I have become truly fond of him and I pray for him every day. I'm sorry he is disappointed now by my activity as pope. I won't say he doesn't have his reasons, but he would be wrong to consider my actions capricious or inspired by ill-will.

ADJUTANT: Why can't the former happy collaboration, which began so promisingly, be resumed? It was good for the kingdom, and also for the Church.

CELESTINE V: For the Church? I doubt that now. You know I donated the tithes of England and France to the king. I appointed some cardinals who were to his satisfaction, in the hope of reducing the arrogance of the great Roman families. And I did him other favours of which I am now, however, less convinced.

ADJUTANT: You regret them? Why? Will you permit me to speak openly?

CELESTINE V: I beg you to.

ADJUTANT: There are those who murmur about Cardinal Caetani's maleficent influence on Your Holiness. He is stirring you up against the king, but at the same time he is not loyal to Your Holiness. In fact, he is already preparing his succession in secret meetings. I can furnish you with the details.

CELESTINE V: They don't interest me. I must tell you I have great respect for Cardinal Caetani, for his learning and for his independence. Our ways of conceiving the Church, however, are opposed. He is in favour of the political supremacy of the papacy, I believe this is no secret; whereas, for me, since you want to know, political power is of no interest.

ADJUTANT: I'll remember that and I am grateful to you for this explanation. You are right, to Caesar must be left what is Caesar's. Still the Church may need the secular arm against heresy. On the other hand, no State would be capable of maintaining public order if its subjects ceased to harbour a holy fear of hell, and this function obviously belongs to the Church. The throne and the altar therefore . . .

CELESTINE V: Don't continue, please. Even you, a soldier, indulge in rhetoric?

ADJUTANT: I was coming to this conclusion: if you don't share Cardinal Caetani's political ambitions, I don't understand why you can't go back to the excellent understanding established with the king at Sulmona.

CELESTINE V: I'll confess the reason to you quite frankly. This is what has happened to me, and if you find it helpful, you can report it to the king: I was elected pope, as you know, just over two months ago, but during the first weeks I was confused by a thousand secondary matters. In a sense, I am slowly becoming pope, and I fear I will never be pope entirely. Perhaps it's impossible to be wholly pope, that is to say, the vicar of Christ. When you think about it, it's an awesome mission. Well, certain actions and gestures I performed during the weeks after my election would be impossible for me to repeat now. In fact, I would do the opposite.

ADJUTANT: I am deeply moved, Your Holiness, at receiving such important confidences from you. My admiration for Your Holiness, which was already great, is immensely increased by them . . . If now, with your permission, I may add a few words, I would like to refer to things of quite a different nature. You know, no doubt, of the negotiations concerning Sicily which your predecessor Nicholas IV carried out with King Charles and with James of Aragon. There is a historical continuity to be safeguarded. Above all, Sicily is under the feudal sovereignty of the Holy See.

CELESTINE V: My first duty, as pope, is to safeguard another continuity, that of the Christian faith. If I were to consent now to some of the king's demands, I would betray it.

ADJUTANT: You refer to his invitation to bless the troops leaving for Sicily?

CELESTINE V: You've guessed it.

ADJUTANT: You know it is a legitimate expedition. You persist in your refusal?

CELESTINE V: At all costs. I repeat to you once and for all: I cannot bless any warlike enterprise. Do you know how Christ's moral teaching can be summed up? You should know it, since you too call yourself a Christian; but I'll remind you, in case you've forgotten. It can be summed up in three words: love one another. Love your neighbour, and also your enemies. We men are all children of the same Father.

ADJUTANT: Your Holiness, no one would wish to censure your thoughts or feelings at the moment you impart your blessing. But for the king, as for the army, it is important that this blessing take place. It will have a significance also for the other rulers of Europe.

CELESTINE V: Try to understand me, I beg you. Even if, in a moment of weakness, I agreed to impart the blessing you ask of me, it would then be physically impossible for me to impart it. Why? My son, it shouldn't be difficult for you to imagine that. The sign of Christian benediction is the Sign of the Cross. You know, don't you, what the Cross is? And the words of the blessing are: in the name of the Father, of the Son, and of the Holy Spirit. If I understand you rightly, you suggest I give this blessing to soldiers about to go off for war, while I am thinking of something else. Did you mean to joke? It would be a horrible sacrilege. With the Sign of the Cross and the names of the Trinity, you can bless bread, soup, oil, water, wine, and if you like, even the tools of labour, the plough, the peasant's hoe, the carpenter's plane, and so on; but not weapons. If you absolutely need some propitiatory rite, find someone who will perform it in the name of Satan. It was he who invented weapons.

ADJUTANT: You know that other popes before you have blessed wars.

CELESTINE V: It is not my place to judge them. I can only pray God to have mercy on them.

[*The adjutant stands up brusquely, gives a stiff military salute and goes off in a great hurry as the stage darkens.*]

LONGING FOR THE HERMIT'S LIFE

When the light returns, Fra Bartolomeo, Fra Angelo, and Fra Ludovico are gathered in the pope's study. Their conversation breaks off, as the first clerk arrives.

FIRST CLERK (*to Fra Angelo*): His Eminence Cardinal Caetani insists that an audience with His Holiness be arranged. It seems he asked for one yesterday, without results.

FRA ANGELO: I still can't give him a precise answer.

FIRST CLERK: Has the request been passed on to His Holiness, at least?

FRA ANGELO: I'll explain. We're in Advent, you know, and though the Holy Father this year has given up his usual retreat of four weeks, he nevertheless devotes more time to the reading of the Holy Books, and to meditation and prayer. We can't go to him on our own initiative; we have to wait until we're called. Fra Ludovico, too, whom you see here and who now belongs to the Celestinian hermits, has been waiting since yesterday to be received. (*After this explanation, the clerk starts to leave, but Fra Angelo invites him to remain.*) You may sit here with us, if you have time.

[*With a brief signal Fra Bartolomeo reassures Fra Ludovico that the clerk can be trusted. Meanwhile, from the square comes a muffled sound of a bagpipe accompanied by a rustic fife. Fra Angelo flings open the balcony door, to hear more readily.*]

FIRST CLERK: This year more bagpipers than usual have come from the Abruzzi. You can see them at every corner and also in front of the little shrines. The bagpipers say they're here to honour the Holy Father, who also came from the same mountains. It would be lovely if, at some point, an echo of their piping reached his ears.

FRA BARTOLOMEO: That happened on the very first evening of Advent, and he was deeply touched by it.

FRA ANGELO: That evening we were talking, in fact, about the

Morrone. He was grieving with us because this year we would spend Christmas without snow and without the music of the shepherds. At that very moment the sound of the bagpipers came up from the square. He sent Fra Bartolomeo down at once to greet them and gave him a present for them.

FRA BARTOLOMEO: They were from Pescocostanzo and as soon as they arrived here they asked people where the pope was.

FRA LUDOVICO: Does our Celestine often recall the Morrone? Does he talk about it with you sometimes?

FRA ANGELO: More and more often, and with frank homesickness. Even his dreams, he told us, take place among the mountains.

FRA BARTOLOMEO: His memory of the earliest years of his hermit life are almost miraculously fresh. Now he often gives way to reminiscences, he tells us odd events and jokes, until he has forgotten the present.

FIRST CLERK (*in a low voice, filled with fervour*): You should make a note of his recollections, I think, so that the memory of them will not be lost.

FRA BARTOLOMEO: It isn't easy to transcribe his way of telling things. For example, there's the story of his first meetings with the vixen, which he later called Suor Giuseppina. Those meetings are like a little fairy-tale. The vixen used to stop at the entrance of his cave and watch him suspiciously, ready to flee at his first movement. "Come in," he would say to her, "what are you afraid of? If you're afraid of me, you're stupid," he said, "yes, downright stupid. They say you're a sly, intelligent animal, but, if you're afraid of me, then there's not a word of truth in it. You ought to understand," he said to her, "if you have any intelligence, that this would be a good opportunity to make a friend. Don't you know what friendship is? Oh, you poor thing, then you're really unfortunate." But the vixen didn't trust his fine words. Until one night Fra Pietro was wakened by some whining, like the yelps of a wounded dog, which were coming from nearby. He got up, looked around, and finally found a vixen, his vixen, caught in a snare set by some shepherd. He freed her, and since in her efforts to free herself, the vixen had been hurt, he tended her as best he could. And so the two became friends. Fra Pietro didn't want to tame her, however. The vixen went on living as before and was always a bit reserved, but she never failed to visit him every evening at the cave. The news of this friendship soon spread among the shepherds of the district and they stopped setting snares to catch the animal.

FRA ANGELO: There's the story of the viper, too. Fra Pietro removed the poison fangs from her jaw and then gave her the name Suor Concettina, because, he said, she seemed a gossip whose tongue has been cut out. But, apart from that, she was a good child. There was the story of the cricket he called Don Cicillo, and other stories, too. Our Fra Bartolomeo also lived in the mountains at that time, not far away from Fra Pietro. When the two of them start telling stories, every now and then, they make you split your sides laughing.

FRA BARTOLOMEO: We also did penance, don't think we didn't. But without melancholy. One morning, when I was passing Fra Pietro's cave, he motioned to me to keep silent. Then later he explained to me that he was so happy that morning because he could hear the grass growing. Other times he would call me to show me a bud that sprouted on a thorn bush. He was ecstatic about it, because he was in the presence of the act of creation.

FRA ANGELO: It would be impossible to lead the hermit's life without being in harmony with nature.

FRA BARTOLOMEO: But, when I think about it, several details of Fra Pietro's life as a hermit remain mysterious to me. For example, he followed sternly the Benedictine rule which divides the day into hours of work and hours of prayer. So, even during the night, he would interrupt his sleep and get up for the prescribed prayers. With all the will in the world, however, I never managed to wake myself up at the right times. On clear nights I could have told the hour by the movement of the stars, but it was a silent indication, and to exercise it, I would have had to be already awake. I asked Fra Pietro to explain his punctuality. "Can't you hear the bell?" he answered. "The first times," he added, "I thought it was you, and it was only later that I realized it must be much nearer my cave." I didn't dare ask him anything further. But he got into the habit, at the beginning of his nightly prayers, of singing a psalm at the top of his voice. So, if the wind was in the right direction, I would wake up too.

[*During all this story, the clerk has been listening, as if spellbound, sitting on the floor next to the monk. As soon as Fra Bartolomeo is silent, Fra Ludovico, who has seemed restless for some while, stands up and paces the room, obviously agitated.*]

FRA LUDOVICO: A man like that . . . A Christian like that . . . Why didn't we oppose his acceptance of the pontificate more strongly? It was an irreparable crime to sacrifice a Christian like him, in this miserable world of ambitious, intriguing rogues. (*To Fra Angelo and Fra Bartolomeo.*) Aren't the two of you tormented with remorse at not having dissuaded him?

FRA ANGELO (*in a low, barely audible voice*): The battle isn't over yet.

FRA LUDOVICO: You can't say that. The battle is already lost, and you two (*nodding also towards Fra Bartolomeo*) know it as well as I. And so does the person chiefly concerned. Otherwise—let's be frank—why all this nostalgia for the Morrone? I'll confess to you that for some time the pope has aroused pity in me. I see him in the Curia like an innocent lamb among arrogant goats. (*Pause.*) Don't you feel the same? What's the use of continuing to pretend?

FRA ANGELO: What conclusion would you like to come to?

FRA LUDOVICO: The wager was lost from the beginning, that's the truth of it. Now it's clear that behind the so-called miraculous election of Perugia there was a deception.

FRA ANGELO (*amazed*): You're still obsessed with that idea? What's the use of talking about it any more?

[*Fra Bartolomeo seems to stir from his lethargy. He stands up and seems about to speak. Then he makes a gesture of resignation and sits down again.*]

FRA ANGELO (*to Fra Ludovico*): Why do you speak of deception? Who was deceived?

FRA LUDOVICO: We were, and, with us, the people of Christ. We deceived ourselves that the election of Fra Pietro meant the rivalries that had made agreement among the cardinals impossible for twenty-seven months had been overcome, and therefore a new epoch in the history of the Church was about to begin. Instead it's now clear that it was only a truce among the old enemies, with no victors and no vanquished. Why that temporary expedient? Since none of the factions was prepared to capitulate, there was no other way out. There were only twelve cardinals, and in every ballot, during all the twenty-seven months, no candidate had ever received more than five votes. They couldn't go on with that little game indefinitely: in Rome, in Spoleto, bloody revolts had broken out, the administration of the Church was paralysed. There was only a temporary solution left: elect to the papacy a good Christian of proved ingenuousness, a man outside the affairs of the world, a meek man who would respect the established interests. To put it bluntly, they wanted to make a pious, unworldly man pope, a man who wouldn't steal and would let the others steal, those who by family tradition, so to speak, had the right. The man who seemed most appropriate for this role was suggested by King Charles the Lame, who has the French art of seduction along with the slyness of the Neapolitans. The cardinals of the opposing factions, naturally reassured in advance, accepted him unanimously and even, like the perfect actors they are, were moved and wept over it. (*Pause.*) But, luckily for Christian honour, our Celestine isn't made of the wood they make their puppets with. (*Pause.*) Where will it end? Have you any idea? I haven't. But I think the deception can't go on much longer.

FIRST CLERK (*deeply upset, rises from the floor, where he was seated*): Forgive me, may I be allowed to speak? Yes, Fra Ludovico, you're unfortunately right in what you say about the Curia. But if the Holy Father could speak directly to the people . . . Ah, you weren't present when he appeared here, for the first time, to the people who were crowding the square and all the streets near by. His simplicity, his meekness, his innocent smile roused that immense crowd to delirious heights. They discovered again, as if in a miraculous vision, the purity and the holiness of Christianity . . . I'll confess to you, these past few days a group of us young people have discussed this matter at length. We're convinced that if the Holy Father addressed the people directly, he could still reverse the situation.

FRA LUDOVICO: My son, you embarrass me. I'm not accustomed to criticize enthusiasm, but now I'm forced to. You see, the enthusiasm of crowds is a straw-fire, especially if it's a festive kind of enthusiasm.

FIRST CLERK: Can't a fire be kindled among men that will last longer than a fire of straw?

FRA LUDOVICO: Well, I'll try to give you an answer. Perhaps I can explain more clearly with an example. There was a fire, not of straw, but a lasting fire which was lighted less than a hundred years ago by Saint Francis of Assisi, and despite the angry efforts of many firemen, it is still burning here and there. Why? Wherever Saint Francis appeared, he didn't invite the people to rejoice and forget their cares, but to be converted, to change their life, to replace the frivolous pleasures of the world with the joys of the spirit, and he set them an example . . . Perhaps what Saint Francis needed to spread his fire through all Christendom, was the help of a pope like Celestine V.

[*During the dialogue between the clerk and Ludovico, the two*

Morronese monks have remained seated, motionless, their eyes on the floor. The room darkens slowly.]

AN UNBEARABLE SITUATION

After a brief pause, the light returns. Celestine V and Cardinal Caetani are seated facing each other.

CELESTINE V: Forgive me for keeping you waiting. It wasn't lack of respect. As you know, I couldn't abolish audiences, so I've reduced their number. Until this year I've always spent Advent in meditation and prayer.

CARD. CAETANI: But now you are pope.

CELESTINE V: Yes, I've learned, to my cost, that it's hard to be pope and remain a good Christian.

CARD. CAETANI: I think it can be done, but in a different way, which is only natural. The higher you rise in the hierarchy of the Church, the more your duties increase and, in consequence, the more your personal freedom is limited.

CELESTINE V: It's exactly as you say. The exercise of command enslaves, starting with those who exercise it. The question is still why there are so many people who would like to command.

CARD. CAETANI: To me, the explanation seems easy. Man longs for command more than for liberty and virtue. Your Holiness, I fear you do not know man.

CELESTINE V: Contempt of man encourages him to be contemptible. The depraved man justifies himself, saying: Isn't this human nature after all? What can I do about it? But the Christian concept of man is noble.

CARD. CAETANI: The concept, yes, but the reality?

CELESTINE V: The reality is varied, I admit. But Christianity calls on man to rise above his animal nature.

CARD. CAETANI: Holy Father, will you allow me to ask an indiscreet question? In your acceptance of the pontificate, did the desire to command play no part at all?

CELESTINE V: In a very confused and even childish way, no doubt it did. I discussed it at length with my confessor and I am doing my penance.

CARD. CAETANI: Forgive my indiscretion and let us talk of other matters. I've heard about your conflict with the king and his military adjutant. I'm delighted. Now I can tell you frankly that there were several of us who were suspicious of your familiarity with the king.

CELESTINE V: The disagreement with the king has made me suffer, because I was and am fond of him. But this conflict has been very helpful to me. If it doesn't seem immodest, I might say I now see a number of important truths more clearly.

CARD. CAETANI: Don't you think some of your previous concessions to the king should be annulled? You've even named him Roman Senator, though our constitution forbids the raising of a king or a reigning prince to that dignity.

CELESTINE V: It was a mistake, I admit. It was ingenuous of me.

CARD. CAETANI: That's how I judge it. No more than that.

CELESTINE V: I grant you the merit, in your relations with the King of Naples, of the greatest coherence of all of us. I learned that, in Perugia, it was you who saved the dignity of the Sacred College by opposing the king's presence in the conclave.

CARD. CAETANI: It was an unheard-of demand, and yet no one dared protest in his presence. Perhaps Your Holiness is unaware how far this king interferes in our affairs. You can form some idea when I tell you that the majority of cardinals receive an annual pension from King Charles. Even some of those who are immensely rich accept it.

CELESTINE V: It's true then that wealth makes men more and more greedy. Aren't the cardinals content with the sale of sinecures?

CARD. CAETANI: We mustn't exaggerate. The trade in sinecures is more talk than substance, and it's difficult to abolish. The practice has ancient traditions behind it. For that matter even corrupt men can be useful. Leave them the freedom of their bad habits, and they can be zealous in the rest.

CELESTINE V: What rest? The restoration of morals?

CARD. CAETANI: Why not? The morals of their adversaries, of course. (*Laughs.*)

CELESTINE V: You laugh? I feel more like crying. (*Pause.*) This morning one of the Colonnas came to me and said to me, quite outspokenly: "You gave the last important concession to the Orsinis, so the next naturally is ours."

CARD. CAETANI: The Colonnas have no manners. For that matter the Orsinis are boasting a bit too much that they have the pope on their side. It seems that an Orsini, some years ago, gave you the funds to build the Abbey of the Holy Spirit at Sulmona.

CELESTINE V: I made no personal use of those funds, and no special obligations were imposed on me.

CARD. CAETANI: I believe you. As for the concessions, I think the wisest course to follow is sensible distributive justice.

CELESTINE V: Wouldn't plain justice, pure and simple, be preferable? But I myself don't see how it can be done.

CARD. CAETANI: The great families are a reality that cannot be ignored.

CELESTINE V: Compared with the greatness of the people of Christ, however, they are very small.

CARD. CAETANI: Anyone familiar with history knows they are the glory and the strength of the Church.

CELESTINE V: If you'll allow me a vulgar expression, they are also her leeches. Don't you agree?

CARD. CAETANI: Those innocent little creatures are sold by druggists, and this means they can also do good. Perhaps the Church, too, needs them. But to whom would you entrust great business matters, if not to the rich families? They're the only ones with the means to carry out such enterprises.

CELESTINE V: And to derive fat profits from them.

CARD. CAETANI: Any business enterprise is a risk, and a risk deserves a reward.

CELESTINE V: And if the reward is exorbitant?

CARD. CAETANI: Have the costs checked.

CELESTINE V: By whom? By their relatives who command the Curia? It would be adding insult to injury, and I don't understand these matters. I come from a poor family. My mother could count only up to five.

CARD. CAETANI: You are fortunate. For the salvation of the soul, poverty is a true stroke of good fortune.

CELESTINE V: You say that in jest?

CARD. CAETANI: I would never dare.

CELESTINE V: But if you seriously consider poverty a favourable condition for the health of the spirit, why don't you renounce your wealth? Isn't the soul the greatest boon?

[*The cardinal looks at the pope in surprise, then bursts out laughing.*]

CARD. CAETANI: You know, there are imbeciles who insist you have no sense of humour?

CELESTINE V: I have at least enough to appreciate your sarcasm now. (*The cardinal starts to add something further to tone down the import of his words, but the pope continues, without paying any attention to him.*) Yes, I admit it was in bad taste for me to take your praise of poverty seriously. But let's go back to our discussion of this so-called distributive justice. My task then would be to divide equally the privileges, the dispensations, the sinecures, the commissions, and the other thieveries among the various factions represented in the Curia. Well, as time goes on, this situation is becoming unbearable to me.

CARD. CAETANI: There's nothing to be done. You tried to change the composition of the Curia, trusting the advice of the king. Have you noticed any improvement after the naming of the new cardinals?

CELESTINE V: None, and I've concluded that the defect lies not so much in the individuals as in the system. The powers of the Curia should be reduced, and the bishops should be given back the powers which they had in the old apostolic times.

CARD. CAETANI (*raises his arms in a gesture of surprise and indignation*): What are you saying? Oh, no, never, no matter what happens. It would be a mortal blow to the Church's unity, already so fragile and unstable. On the contrary, Your Holiness, on the contrary, the Church needs more than ever to remain united, to defend her prerogatives, and to dominate princes and states. Don't you realize that if we granted the French bishops autonomy, we would soon lose them?

CELESTINE V: That may be, but the absolute dominion of the Roman Curia seems even more pernicious to me, because it is repelling the men of good will throughout Christendom.

CARD. CAETANI (*still burning with scorn*): It's a pity you didn't reveal these thoughts publicly before the vote of the conclave, and a greater pity that none of us was able, even remotely, to foresee them.

CELESTINE V (*smiling*): Will you believe me if I assure you there was no dissembling on my part? It's only recently, looking around as pope, that I've come to these conclusions. Now, you say that if you and the other cardinals had been able to foresee it, your votes would have been different? I, too, am convinced of that. No one, however, not even the Sacred College, can limit the freedom of the Holy Spirit. What he has done, He can undo, without waiting for me to die.

CARD. CAETANI (*with unconcealed eagerness*): Holy Father, what do you mean?

CELESTINE V: You will know, explicitly, very soon, and you will receive a great personal joy.

[*The cardinal smiles and, in an irresistible burst of gratitude, kneels at the feet of the pope, who gives him his blessing. Darkness.*]

THE GREAT REFUSAL

When the light returns, Fra Bartolomeo, Fra Angelo, and Fra Ludovico are busily preparing the room for the imminent consistory. Fra Angelo places neatly on the table the purple mantle, the stole and the tiara the pope will wear for his allocution to the cardinals. Fra Bartolomeo and Fra Ludovico carefully set an armchair on a dais, as a kind of throne, near the entrance to the hall. The action proceeds in silence; the expression of the three monks is serious and concerned. The first clerk appears in the doorway, carrying a small armchair.

FIRST CLERK (*to Fra Angelo*): Where do the little armchairs go?

FRA ANGELO: Not here. They should be lined up in the great hall. They're for the cardinals.

FIRST CLERK: Isn't one needed next to the Holy Father's throne?

FRA ANGELO: He said that, on this occasion, he wants only people he trusts next to him: so no cardinals. Stay with me, you three, he said, and, if they like, also the two little clerks.

[*The second clerk comes in, almost running, very anxious and upset.*]

SECOND CLERK: It is true that the Holy Father plans to abdicate?

[*No one answers him. The clerk, sadly, feels his news is confirmed, and he bursts into sobs.*]

FIRST CLERK (*goes over to speak to him in a low voice*): There's nothing to be done now, you know. I'll explain to you later.

SECOND CLERK: How can it be? It's maddening. Such a thing has never happened before.

FIRST CLERK: You're right, never before. But the cardinals will make no objection, you'll see.

SECOND CLERK: No, the cardinals won't. I should think not. But what about all good Christians? So the Holy Father is going to abandon us? Is such a thing possible? Isn't he running away?

FRA LUDOVICO (*who has heard the excited protest of the clerk*): No, my son, he isn't running away. His is an act of courage, an act of loyalty to himself and to others.

SECOND CLERK: A thing like this has never happened before.

FRA LUDOVICO: That isn't exactly correct. In the history of the Church the word *never* is out of place. Everything that is humanly possible, has already happened. The only super-human fact is that the Church still exists.

SECOND CLERK: There's a question I've already heard others ask: can someone elected by the Holy Spirit renounce his throne? Did the Holy Spirit make a mistake?

FRA LUDOVICO: No, He's infallible. But can't this abdication also be inspired by Him?

[*The king's military adjutant bursts into the room, and since those present pay no attention to him, he addresses them all in a loud voice.*]

ADJUTANT: I have been sent by His Majesty to invite the Holy Father for an urgent discussion, at the Royal Palace, or here, as His Holiness prefers.

FRA ANGELO: The august request will be brought to His Holiness's attention as soon as possible.

ADJUTANT: His Majesty is awaiting an immediate reply.

FRA ANGELO: It will be immediate, obviously, as soon as His Holiness has received the request.

[*The adjutant strides towards the cloistered cell, but Fra Ludovico is ahead of him and bars the way.*]

FRA LUDOVICO: I warn you we will tolerate no bullying.

[*After a moment's reflection, the adjutant hastily retraces his steps. Through the doorway some prelates can be seen, and other figures who have rushed in to hear a confirmation or denial of the sensational news of the abdication. Fra Bartolo-meo keeps them at bay and prevents them from entering the antechamber. In the resultant murmuring, a few isolated exclamations can be distinguished.*]

VOICES: "How can it be? Has such a thing ever happened?"

"So it's true then? Good God, what times we live in!"

"Did the Holy Spirit make a mistake in Perugia, or is He making a mistake now? Eh, it has to be one or the other. *Aut aut.*"

"The last word—wait and see—will come from the Sorbonne."

[*Fra Bartolomeo opens the door slightly and remains there on guard, with the two clerks, to keep outsiders from entering. But almost immediately Cardinal Caetani arrives, and he is promptly allowed to pass. Before going on, he stops for a friendly word with the two clerks.*]

FRA ANGELO (*to Fra Ludovico*): There's the future pope. He's procured the support of the Orsinis, so he already has a majority in the Sacred College. Unlike the Perugia conclave, the next conclave will be one of the shortest in the history of the Church.

CARD. CAETANI (*advances into the antechamber and calls Fra Ludovico to him*): Is the Holy Father in his cell?

FRA ANGELO: Yes, but we can't disturb him.

CARD. CAETANI: Of course not. He now needs calm and meditation more than ever.

FRA LUDOVICO: Don't worry. We've never seen him more serene than in these past few days.

CARD. CAETANI: So much the better. Tell him then, from me, that he need fear no opposition from the consistory. The majority favours silent acceptance of the declaration he and I agreed on.

FRA ANGELO: And what will the minority do?

CARD. CAETANI: They're puzzled, without a leader, and they'll be silent. The real danger lies outside the consistory.

FRA ANGELO: The king has sent to ask the Holy Father for an urgent audience.

CARD. CAETANI: I hope he'll refuse it, at least until after the ceremony. When he's faced with the hard facts, the king sooner or later will resign himself, even if some of his advisers are suggesting insane actions to him.

FRA LUDOVICO: What advisers and what insane actions?

CARD. CAETANI: Since the first news of the abdication, the Colonna camp has been in a state of real hysteria. Perhaps you know, they're adventurers without any scruples, capable of any misdeed. Some of them now have suddenly become theologians and they go around blathering that the abdication will be annulled and the new conclave will be illegal. On the pretext of saving the religious peace of the kingdom, they have asked the king to use force to prevent it.

FRA ANGELO: Does the king agree?

CARD. CAETANI: He hasn't agreed so far. He's asked advice of Paris and this may have serious consequences.

FRA LUDOVICO: Not for our Celestine surely. From this evening on, he will be out of the fight.

CARD. CAETANI: Don't deceive yourselves. If the French bishops refuse to recognize the abdication, it might cause a schism. We would have two popes, Celestine V and the one elected by the new conclave.

FRA ANGELO: There's no fear our Celestine would lend himself to such a manœuvre.

CARD. CAETANI: The French—you know them—can do without his consent. They could seize him, isolate him and take him to Lyons or somewhere else, keeping him ignorant of the consequences.

FRA ANGELO: Don't you think this view contains too many "if's" ... If the king of Naples ... If the French bishops... If the next conclave ... We already have enough to worry about, just to live through this day.

CARD. CAETANI: You're right. But it isn't premature to think where Celestine will go this evening or tomorrow, when he leaves this palace. A hermit can sleep even under bridges, but not a pope, or an ex-pope.

FRA ANGELO: We thought . . .

FRA LUDOVICO (*interrupts him, distrusting the cardinal*): We haven't thought about that yet.

CARD. CAETANI: Tell him my house in Anagni is at his disposal.

He will be safe there and will want for nothing. In any case, to spare him great trouble, from now on we had better act in agreement and with discretion.

FRA ANGELO: Naturally I will report your every word to the Holy Father.

[*Vague voices and sounds come from the adjacent hall.*]

CARD. CAETANI: The cardinals are beginning to arrive. Don't allow anyone to enter this room.

[*The two monks bow briefly as the cardinal goes back into the great hall.*]

FRA LUDOVICO: With all due discretion, I think we agree: neither Anagni nor Lyons.

FRA ANGELO: It's obvious: no frying-pan and no fire. Our plan for Celestine remains the same.

[*From the square comes a growing sound of a popular demonstration, in which sacred hymns are united to cries of "Long live . . ." and "Down with . . ." The monks and clerks run to the balcony.*]

FRA BARTOLOMEO: What is it? What's happening?

FIRST CLERK: It must be the procession for the feast of Saint Lucy. Today's the 13th of December.

SECOND CLERK: The Saint Lucy procession has never passed this way before. How strange.

[*The meaning of the procession's unusual route begins to grow more clear as soon as it approaches the papal residence. At a certain point the cries seem to come from inside the palace. The door on the right of the papal antechamber, the one reserved for the king and high court dignitaries, is suddenly flung open. For a moment the king's adjutant appears there, but he immediately withdraws to open the way to a group of ragged poor people, clustered around a banner with the image of Saint Lucy. The intruders come just beyond the threshold of the door. The people already present in the room immediately form a barrier before the entrance to the cell; while, from the opposite side, from the hall where the cardinals have gathered, Cardinal Caetani appears. After a rapid glance to see what is happening, he draws back, shutting the door after him. The man with the banner takes a step forward and shouts:*

"*Long live Saint Lucy, long live the pope, long live the king.*"

The shout is echoed by his companions, who wave their caps in the air. Somebody revises the cry, and the others shout his new version:

"*Long live the pope and down with the cardinals.*"

All eyes are fixed on the little door of the cell. It opens, and the tall, solemn figure of the pope appears. All present, including the intruders, greet him with a brief genuflexion; only the two clerks remain on their knees. The pope seems in pain, but serene; he proceeds slowly to the centre of the room and stands in front of the group of poor people. The flag-bearer raises his banner and repeats, in chorus with his companions:

"*Long live Saint Lucy, long live the pope, long live the king.*"]

CELESTINE V (*in a tired, mild voice*): Who led you here? How did you reach that door, which is reserved for the king?

FLAG-BEARER: Holy Father, we want to speak to you in the name of the people. Stay with us. Don't abandon us. Don't abandon your flock to the wolves.

SECOND MAN: Send away the cardinals and stay with the people and the king.

THIRD MAN: The cardinals are the ruination of the Church, just as the barons are the ruination of the kingdom. Don't leave us.

THE INTRUDERS (*together*): Holy Father, free the Church of the Roman Curia.

FOURTH MAN: If you hand them over to us, Your Holiness, we'll free you from those rascally cardinals.

CELESTINE V: How dare you speak words of violence in the

pope's presence? (*Pause.*) Listen to me. If a person has gangrene in an arm or a leg, he can be saved if the afflicted part is cut away. But if the disease has spread to many parts of the body, there can be no cutting.

FLAG-BEARER: What can be done in that case?

CELESTINE V: Let us pray together. Repeat after me each sentence I speak. I'll be brief. (*Joining his hands, the pope begins his prayer.*) Our Father who art in heaven, on earth and in all places . . .

POPULACE and RELIGIOUS PRESENT: Our Father who art in heaven, on earth and in all places . . .

CELESTINE V: Thy kingdom come . . .

OTHERS: Thy kingdom come . . .

CELESTINE V: Now I'll give you my blessing. (*With his right arm he makes the Sign of the Cross in the air, while the poor people also cross themselves.*) And now, please, go with God and try to be good.

[*The poor people withdraw and Fra Bartolomeo hastens to shut the door after them. The pope notices that the two clerks have remained kneeling and one of them is unable to hide his tears.*]

CELESTINE V: My dear children, rise. I hope this little incident hasn't upset you. (*He bends to help them stand up.*)

SECOND CLERK (*barely able to restrain his sobs*): Holy Father, even if those men expressed themselves in crude words, they represent the feelings of the majority of the faithful. Listen to the people, Your Holiness. *Vox populi, vox Dei.*

[*In the meanwhile the noise of the crowd gathered below the windows of the palace breaks out again with greater violence, perhaps because they have been informed of the useless conversation of their representatives with the pope.*]

CELESTINE V (*to the two clerks*): I love the people, but not with a blind love. I too come from the people, and I know them well. They can easily be deceived, aroused, misled. Have you wondered who told that crowd of my decision? And how was it explained to them? Who gave orders to shift the Saint Lucy procession from its traditional route and bring it under my windows? No, it isn't true that the voice of the people is always the voice of God. Don't forget that it was the people who asked for the liberation of Barabbas and the crucifixion of Christ. What can the people know of the terrible examination of conscience I have had to make in these past few days? We must love the people, but no uproar of the crowd must ever prevail over the voice of the conscience. Of course, my children, I'm sorry to have to go far away from you and never see you again.

FIRST CLERK: Take us with you.

SECOND CLERK: Don't abandon us. Allow us to follow you.

CELESTINE V: To follow me where? The short time left me, my children . . . I'd like to spend in peace, in some cave of the Maiella, far from intrigues, from rivalries, from envy and greed. . . . Peace, that's all I want.

FRA ANGELO: Holy Father, I'll take care of these two young friends of ours.

[*The pope nods his consent, and since the din of the crowd shows no sign of dying down, he motions to Fra Bartolomeo to shut the blinds of the balcony and draw the curtains. The outside noises cease, and since it is now almost dark, Fra Angelo and Fra Ludovico light the tapers in the various candelabra. In the crypt-like penumbra the pontifical robing takes place quickly. The pope is assisted by Fra Bartolomeo and by Fra Angelo, who hand him the ring, the purple mantle, the stole and the mitre.*]

CELESTINE V: My brothers, let us waste no more time. I'm ready.

[*Fra Ludovico flings open the door to the room where the cardinals are gathered and the pope takes his place on the throne. Fra Bartolomeo and Fra Angelo kneel at either side of him; Fra Ludovico and the two clerks a bit behind. Absolute silence reigns. The pope's face is illuminated by the intense light from the great hall.*]

CELESTINE V (*in a loud voice*): Peace be with you.
CARDINALS (*in a loud voice*): And with thy spirit.
CELESTINE V: Let us pray.

[*At the end of the silent prayer, the pope makes the Sign of the Cross.*]

CELESTINE V: My brothers in Christ, you know already why this extraordinary consistory has been called. So I need make no exordium and I can say only what is strictly necessary. I will not speak, therefore, about the root of the matter, about what I think of the situation of the Church in the world of today, because it isn't a question that can be resolved here and now. I have not had the opportunity of facing it, nor are you capable of resolving it, nor do I see anyone else, among the men of today, who can do so. So I will speak to you only of myself and of the act which I am about to carry out, and I beg you to hear me in silence, to spare me interruptions, questions, comments, protests, and pleas. At least in this meeting, let us try to be charitable and loyal with one another.

[*Fra Angelo hands the pope a folder in which the Formula of Abdication is written.*]

VOICE FROM THE HALL: Most blessed Father . . .
CELESTINE V: I asked you to listen, without asking questions.
SAME VOICE: This isn't a question, it's a suggestion, to make your act conform to canon law.
CELESTINE V: Who are you?
VOICE: Matteo Orsini.
CELESTINE V: Speak then.
MATTEO ORSINI: Most blessed Father, since you are firm in your intention, let your will be done. However, if you wish your renunciation to be ratified and stable, define first of all, with a special constitution, that the pope can for legitimate cause renounce the papacy and the cardinals can accept his renunciation.
CELESTINE V: So be it. I ask you to formulate yourself this new

principle and, by the authority which at this moment I still retain, I accept and decree it as law. (*He opens the folder given him by Fra Angelo and reads in a loud, slow voice.*) Hear me: I, Celestine, moved by legitimate reasons, by need of humility, of moral perfection, and by the obligation of my conscience, as well as by physical weakness, by lack of doctrine and by the wickedness of the world, in order to recover the peace and the consolations of my former way of life,

with all my heart, freely resign from the papacy. I expressly renounce the throne, the dignity, the charge, and the honour,

giving at this moment free and full power to the Sacred College of cardinals to choose and provide, by due canonical procedure, the new pastor of the Universal Church.

[*When the reading is finished, murmurs and exclamations rise from the hall, vigorously silenced by the majority of those present. The abdicating pope descends from the throne and, before all the cardinals, he removes the ring, the mitre, the stole, and the mantle, setting them on the floor near him. With the help of Fra Ludovico he then puts on once more the rough habit of the hermits. After which Fra Bartolomeo shuts the door and Celestine walks in silence to his cell.*]

FRA ANGELO (*to Fra Ludovico*): Now we can say that we have witnessed the end of a strange story.

FRA LUDOVICO: This isn't the end yet, I fear. (*To the audience.*) Be patient just a little longer. This isn't the end.

[*Darkness.*]

[END OF PART TWO]

IV

Sulmona. January, 1295

THE DOUBLE SEARCH FOR PIER CELESTINE

While the stage is still half-dark and deserted, the sound of a town-crier's trumpet is heard, muffled by the distance; the blasts are followed by the reading of a proclamation, of which only a few isolated phrases are audible. "The new pope Boniface . . . the ex-pope Celestine . . . order for his capture . . .", greeted by hostile jeers and other noises from the public. After a while, the crier himself appears on the stage, entering backwards, rapidly; it is Cerbicca, whom we have already met. He is dressed in his usual outlandish, bizarre way, holding the trumpet in one hand and, with the other, dragging a sack already half full. Cerbicca is followed by jeers and protests and by cabbage-stalks, turnips and rotten apples and pears hurled by people who can't be seen because of the darkness. Cerbicca collects and puts in his sack anything that seems even slightly edible among the objects thrown at him.

CERBICCA (*makes a clumsy bow towards his invisible audience*): Thank you, most generous admirers. I thank you from the bottom of my heart for your warm reception and for your gifts. While we're on that subject, I would only like to suggest you send me, if possible, fewer cabbage stalks and more turnips. If it's all the same to you, naturally.

[*After having drunk a sip, perhaps of brandy, from a little bottle he extracts from a secret pocket, he blows his trumpet again, allows the people of the neighbourhood time to appear at the windows or come down into the street and then, in a stentorian voice, he repeats his announcement.*]

CERBICCA: The noble citizenry of Sulmona is informed that His Majesty the King of Naples and His Holiness the new Pope Boniface (*this name inspires a few boos and the throwing of some vegetables*) . . . as I was saying, these two important personages—you can think what you like about them, I don't care—are very worried because they don't know where the devil the ex-pope Celestine is or what in the world he's up to, since he ran away from Naples in the dead of the night, as you well know, leaving no address. (*Shouts of "clown", "buffoon", "spy", and the hurling of more stalks interrupt the crier again.*) As I was saying, they're very worried that the French may steal our beloved Celestine, and so they want Celestine to be caught, wherever he may be, and handed over, whether he likes it or not, to our legitimate authorities who will take care to put him in a safe place in one of our prisons where, as many of us well know, you're better off than anywhere else, especially as far as filth is concerned. (*A turnip strikes the crier's head and makes him stagger; however, a moment later he continues unperturbed.*) Now comes the most important part, so pay attention, for your own good and the good of your family. Anybody, inspired by noble Christian and patriotic sentiments, who turns informer and helps in the capture of the aforesaid Celestine, will receive a reward . . . (*the shouts of his listeners make the description of the reward inaudible*) . . . whereas any coward who, in one way or another, helps Celestine hide, will be locked up in jail.

[*The end of the edict arouses, against Cerbicca, a new shower of garbage and other solid refuse, which he carefully examines for the same reason as before. Then he steps to the footlights and sits on the ground, trumpet and sack on either side of him.*]

CERBICCA (*to the audience*): I hope you've admired my skill as acting town-crier, with something to say for each side, even though my real profession, you know, is landowner. The titular town-crier, whose place I've taken, is sick—or so he insists. He was fine until he read today's edict; then he suddenly turned pale and lost his voice. He said (*Cerbicca imitates a hoarse voice*): "I'd do it gladly, but

I can't, on my word of honour, I can't. You hear me? I've lost my voice." Strange illness. Like the town-crier, there are a lot of other people here who have strangely lost their voices these past few days. Among them is the pastor, Don Costantino, whom you also know. He was to read the edict from the pulpit. (*Cerbicca again imitates someone who has lost his voice.*) "I can't," he answered, "I've lost my voice; can't you hear I've lost my voice?" The edict was affixed to the doors of the churches, by order of the Grand Justiciary; but it didn't stay long on any of the doors. They probably didn't use good glue in sticking it up. Strange glue. All these strange things may be explained by the fact that, until a few weeks ago, the same gentlemen who are now organizing the hunt for our Celestine were shouting his praises to the skies. Nobody has forgotten the spectacle, just three or four months ago, when he set out from here with the procession for l'Aquila, for the solemn papal coronation. Astride a donkey, with the king on one side and the crown prince on the other, holding the reins, he was confused and shy, like you or I would have been in his place. For the people around here the new pope became another Jesus Christ, the Celestine monks suddenly became the lords of the manor; they were the ones, unfortunately, who laid down the law. Since I see you're anxious to know what I think about it, I'll tell you in just a few words. Pier Celestine—as he's called now—is a creature that, frankly, you can't help loving. Perhaps—or rather, no perhaps about it—he's crazy, but he's lovably crazy. I'd rather not speak about his monks, however. And yet, at one point, I tried to worm my way into their good graces. Unfortunately, if a man is involved in big business, as I am, unless he's stupid, he joins up with those who give the orders. So one evening I went to a meeting for the formation of a new Confraternity, which was held in the courtyard of a convent, and I had resigned myself to becoming a part of it. First of all, a Celestine monk made us a speech about the Kingdom of God in this world, which to his way of thinking was about to be set up. I don't mind telling you, it was a fine speech, full of quotations from the prophets; and plenty of those present were crying. Well, it was one of those speeches where the less the listeners understand, the harder they cry. As soon as we came to the questions and answers part, I stood up, and with the common sense of a true landowner, I asked for a few practical explanations. "In the Kingdom of God which, according to you, is almost ready to come about," I asked the preacher, "will we eat? What will we eat? And will the food be free or will it cost money?" They wouldn't even let me finish my questions; a couple of hefty monks picked me up bodily and threw me out of the courtyard. It's easy to understand that they acted so brutally just because they didn't know how to answer me; but I haven't forgotten that insult. This is one of the reasons why, when I heard the authorities were looking for a town-crier and couldn't find one, because anybody they asked around here promptly lost his voice, I stepped right up. "I learned to play the trumpet," I said, "when I was in the army, and when I've had something to drink, I also have a fine voice." But, in the back of my mind, as I'll freely admit to you, there was another reason, besides my dislike of those monks. I must tell you that, ever since I was a child, I've had one great ambition: to become a beadle. In itself, as you'll point out to me, this isn't anything original because, to speak frankly, who wouldn't like to become a beadle? Now I thought in fact that, acting as town-crier in this delicate situation, I would gain the benevolence of the authorities and would make a great step towards the position of beadle which for me, as for any sensible man, remains an enviable goal. The same cannot be said, however, for other positions which were formerly preferred; for example, you couldn't say that about the papacy. Until a few weeks ago, we had a saying "to live like a pope", which meant to live very well. Or the expression "tonight I feel like a pope", which meant the man who said it had eaten and drunk his fill and was without troubles or problems of any kind. But now, after our Pier Celestine has gone off, slamming the door of the Holy See, you can't talk like that any more, even if it's not clear just why he resigned. Here they can talk about nothing else, though nobody knows anything exactly; however, they say, if a pious man, with a good character like that, has gone off, somehow or other they must have treated him badly. Maybe they didn't give him enough to eat, or else they cut his wages; these are the most popular guesses. Whatever happened, one thing is certain: nowadays even the job of pope has its drawbacks. Still, nobody expected the worst, and now it's come. Among my friends in high places, such as the pastor Don Costantino, I've heard this question asked: Why, after having accepted Celestine's resignation, is the new pope now hunting him down? Nobody around here believes those stories about the French. They make other suppositions. Maybe, after Celestine had left, they realized some silverware was missing from the papal palaces, and they talk about the French rather than report the scandal. If this is true, to my way of thinking, the fault lies with his monks. But if the new pope has proof that Celestine himself is the guilty party then, according to me, there would be just one explanation: the holy man did it in a moment of absent-mindedness. When you're tying up a bundle of linen or dirty clothes, you can easily wrap up a silver candlestick or other valuable objects inside it. A little oversight of the sort happened to me once, and it must have happened to many of you . . .

[*Suddenly from the darkness at the rear of the stage the gendarme, whom we already know, arrives and hurries menacingly to Cerbicca.*]

GENDARME: We might have expected as much from a rascal like you. Now the whole city is laughing over your edict.

CERBICCA: Did you want them to cry?

GENDARME: They're not laughing at you, you good-for-nothing. They're laughing at the authorities, that's the trouble. Why didn't you just read the words of the edict, instead of changing them like a fool?

CERBICCA: I didn't read it—if I may speak in confidence and if you'll keep this to yourself—because I'm illiterate. If I knew how to read and write, I wouldn't be a land-owner. I'd be a poet.

GENDARME: You could have memorized it, at least.

CERBICCA: If I had a good enough memory to learn a rigmarole as long as that, I'd be a preacher or a lawyer.

GENDARME: Then I can't understand why you were so insistent on having the parchment with the words of the edict.

CERBICCA: Can't you guess? Any man who loves cleanliness will always find some use for a sheet of parchment. Besides, before using it, I had the pastor Don Costantino explain to me carefully what was written in it, and I repeated it faithfully.

GENDARME: Faithfully, my foot. You've stupidly compromised the whole campaign of the authorities. But to speak of decorum with you is like talking about music with a deaf man.

CERBICCA: If the authorities set so much store by decorum, then they should understand it's impossible to make decorous propaganda against Celestine here, in the Morrone and Maiella district, where he is venerated by one and all. They should make their propaganda in other cities, where he's unknown.

GENDARME: Don't talk nonsense. In cities where he's unknown, propaganda would be useless.

CERBICCA: Useless, perhaps, but decorous.

GENDARME: I don't know why I'm wasting my time arguing with such a thick-headed imbecile. Celestine is hidden around these parts, that much is certain, and the authorities have orders to capture him.

CERBICCA: Can't you realize you'll never catch him? Here he's defended not only by the inhabitants, but also by the stones, the trees, the grass of the mountains. So, when you don't capture him, after all this trumpeting and edicts, the authorities' decorum will suffer shamefully. Whereas, if they hunted for him somewhere else, where he surely isn't, their decorum would be saved, because no honest person could criticize them for not finding him.

GENDARME: How can you invent such foolishness?

CERBICCA (*haughtily*): You're in no position to judge, gendarme; that's up to your superiors. In reporting my ideas, you may add that I have other, even more original ideas, you might say ideas of genius. As for you, once and for all, I must warn you that if you don't listen to my advice you'll never become a general.

GENDARME (*annoyed*): In any case your job as town-crier is over. (*He picks up the trumpet and starts to go off.*)

CERBICCA (*shrugs indifferently*): So much the better for me. After all, it was humiliating for a landowner to go around the streets playing a trumpet.

GENDARME (*comes back*): What's this constant boast of yours about being a landowner? Where are your fields?

CERBICCA: I never mentioned any fields. I simply stated my profession. There's a difference.

GENDARME: So you are, so to speak, a property-owner without any property.

CERBICCA: What a hard head you have. I repeat: since I was unable to become beadle, I chose the profession of landowner. But, as I don't have any fields, I am not practising my profession. I am, you might say, a landowner on leave.

[*Darkness.*]

THE DUTY TO RESIST PERSECUTION

The light returns. A chasm can be seen, between high, steep cliffs. Pier Celestine, Fra Bartolomeo and Fra Angelo are seated on large boulders, waiting for some friends. They wear the usual Morronese habit. After a little while, one by one, cautiously, Fra Clementino and the two Neapolitan ex-clerks arrive. The two youths now wear the habit of Celestine novices.

FRA CLEMENTINO (*hands Pier Celestine an ancient codex*): It's a gift from Fra Ludovico, a remembrance for the time of separation which, he fears, may be long.

PIER CELESTINE (*after examining the frontispiece of the codex, clasping it to his heart*): *The Concordance of the Old and the New Testaments* by Joachim of Fiore? What a wonderful and providential gift.

FRA BARTOLOMEO (*to Fra Clementino*): Isn't Fra Ludovico coming? Are we to wait for him?

FRA CLEMENTINO (*to Pier Celestine*): Fra Ludovico and the other friars who have stayed with him dare not come, for reasons of prudence. From morning to night, they're being followed by strange men who certainly belong to the secret police.

PIER CELESTINE: I'm pleased Fra Ludovico knows also how to be prudent. I was worried because of his impetuousness. (*To the two older monks.*) I believe these young people (*pointing to Fra Clementino and the two novices*) must be authorized to strip themselves of the habit and dress in such a way that they can pass unobserved. What names have the two novices taken?

FIRST EX-CLERK: My name now is Luca.

SECOND EX-CLERK: Mine is Gioacchino.

PIER CELESTINE (*to the two*): If you want to follow a normal novitiate, you must enter the Abbey of the Holy Spirit. I don't believe Boniface will dare close it, at most he'll take away some of its privileges.

LUCA (*after consulting Gioacchino*): We'd rather stay with you, or at least remain at your orders, to be of what help we can. If that isn't possible, we'll go back to Naples.

PIER CELESTINE (*smiles*): I thank you. It will be a rather hard apprenticeship, but perhaps not boring. (*To the two older monks.*) Are we waiting for anyone else?

FRA BARTOLOMEO: Matteo the weaver ought to be coming too.

GIOACCHINO: He's not well. (*To Fra Bartolomeo.*) He asked me to tell you that some of the duties assigned him are being carried out by his daughter, Concetta.

FRA BARTOLOMEO: That reassures me. Concetta is an intelligent and courageous girl.

GIOACCHINO: Yes, an unusual girl. And if she needs help, she can also call on two other girls, friends of hers.

[*An icy wind rises, penetrating even into the chasm. The older monks put up their hoods.*]

FRA ANGELO (*observes the sky*): The snow is late, but that isn't a good sign. We'll have a severe winter this year.

FRA CLEMENTINO: May I gather some brush and light a fire?

FRA BARTOLOMEO: You'd make more smoke than fire, and the smoke would be seen far away. In the coming months the cold will be our worst enemy.

PIER CELESTINE: I'm grieved for you, but it isn't necessary for these boys to stay in the mountains. I'd gladly send them to pass the winter in Apulia, halfway to Greece, where they could keep in touch with our exiles. It's a plan we should consider. As for myself, let me say this: any penance will seem to me deserved.

LUCA AND GIOACCHINO: Deserved?

PIER CELESTINE: I'm not referring to Boniface's present persecution. It's stupid and unjust, like all actions inspired by fear. When an ambitious and weak man is seized with panic, he inevitably sees dangers everywhere and falls back on the most absurd falsehoods. If Boniface were able to think clearly, he would immediately realize he has nothing to fear from me.

FRA ANGELO: Couldn't we try to persuade him of his error? Someone of us who knew him when he was cardinal . . .

PIER CELESTINE: I've already tried, but in vain. Now we have only one duty: with God's help, we must resist injustice. It is a sacrosanct Christian duty, not to surrender to persecution. (*Pause.*) The cause of my sufferings, dear children, is, however, something else. I feel I must speak of it to you, as if in confession, divesting myself of all self-love. My soul is torn with remorse. You know its origin. Why did I accept that election? Why did I allow its meaning to be inflated beyond all measure? Why did I deceive so many good Christians, and first of all yourselves, my dear sons, allowing you to believe the conditions existed for a total renovation of the life of the Church? Why didn't I understand that, apart from all the rest, my physical strength would have been insufficient even for an ordinary pontificate? (*Some of those present want to interrupt this bitter confession.*) No, let me speak. There is only one thing that can attenuate my guilt: my ignorance. I became aware of all my many grave sins and aberrations too late, and too slowly. If I may tell you the whole truth, I feel I still haven't reached the end of my examination of conscience and I pray God to let me live at least long enough to complete it. (*Pause.*) I faced the venture like a blindfolded donkey. I assure you that the comparison isn't an exaggeration. Would you like to know my greatest worry in the days of my acceptance? My ignorance of the liturgy. How will I manage, I asked myself, in the great pontifical ceremonies in the basilicas of Rome? What foolishness. Yes, that too was a difficulty, of course, but it was a trifle compared to the others. (*Pause.*) In serious questions, I thought I could be clever. There is nothing more ridiculous than a simpleton who believes he can be clever. I thought I could make use of the king "to good ends". That cursed phrase "to good ends". My sons, don't forget: there is only good, pure and simple. There are no "good ends". (*Pause.*) Now I'm ashamed of everything I did for good ends, for example, my sly tricks to take possession of the Benedictine monastery at Cassino. And of other things, many other things of that sort. I was truly stupid. (*Pause.*) Make use of power? What a pernicious illusion. It's power that makes use of us. Power is a difficult horse to lead: it goes where it must go, or rather, it goes where it can go or

where it's natural for it to go. You can't ask a horse to
fly: if it doesn't fly, you can't blame it. You have to be
content with the satisfaction of sitting on his back. The
same can be said of the Roman Curia: it is what it is. (*Pause.*)
The ambition to command, the obsession with power is, on
all levels, a form of madness. It devours the soul, over-
whelms it, makes it false. Even if you aspire to power "to
good ends"—*especially* if you aspire to power "to good
ends". The temptation of power must be the most diabolical that can be held out to man, if Satan dared propose
it even to Christ. With Christ he didn't succeed, but he
succeeds with Christ's vicars. It's a more treacherous
temptation than the weakness of the senses. In fact, many
chaste men succumb to it. (*Pause.*) All in all, mine was a
sad adventure, the most painful time of my life. At the
beginning I felt caught up in a whirlpool. Later the tor-
ment began: I had to make gestures I didn't want to make,
say words I didn't mean, sign documents I didn't understand, drawn up by others according to their personal
convenience, bulls were in circulation bearing my signature
though I hadn't signed them. Everyone stole, some more,
some less, even those who came to me to report the thefts of
the others. (*Pause.*) I lived at court, as I do here, the life of
a humble beggar. But what good did that do? It just made
the Monsignors laugh.

GIOACCHINO: Luca and I didn't laugh.

PIER CELESTINE: No. You were my consolation and I am in-
finitely grateful to you. Young people like you are my hope
now.

FRA ANGELO: There are few of us left. Many who were with us
at the moment of triumph have abandoned us now.

PIER CELESTINE: It may be that others, in their consciences, are
with us now and we don't even know them.

GIOACCHINO: Mustn't we fear that, in the face of these persecutions, their kind will dwindle and die out?

PIER CELESTINE: No, frankly I don't fear that. There will always
be some Christians who will take Christ seriously, some

absurd Christian, as Boniface likes to say. Since even those who betray Him can't destroy the Gospel. They can hide it, they can invent comfortable interpretations of it, but they can't destroy it. So from time to time someone will rediscover it and will be ready to put himself in jeopardy, with his soul serene.

FRA CLEMENTINO: What about us? We can't simply go to sleep, trusting that there will always be honest and courageous Christians. In our present state, what can we do?

PIER CELESTINE: Well, it seems to me that, first of all, we have the duty of the housewife who, at night, covers the embers on the hearth with ashes, so she can light the fire more easily the next morning. And then we will have the constant task of maintaining links among ourselves and encouraging our scattered friends. When a net is ripped apart, it has to be sewn together all over again. We must create a foothold in the Gargano for communication with the exiles.

FRA BARTOLOMEO: How long will our communication last before the authorities destroy it?

PIER CELESTINE: I don't know. But when it's suppressed in one place, it can spring up somewhere else.

FRA CLEMENTINO: You know, if the night is long, the embers under the ash can go out. How many years will this night last? The night that Christ's Church is going through?

PIER CELESTINE: My son, how can I know that? Many years went by before Christ was born. Perhaps, before she can rise again, the Church will have to rot away completely. There is a mystery of the Church that our minds cannot penetrate. But it's important that a certain number of Christians keep alive, in themselves, what seems premature for the rest of the world.

GIOACCHINO: You mean that for the present we must concern ourselves with our own soul? We must cultivate it the way some people cultivate their garden? But in this way aren't we forgetting the Kingdom of God, announced by the Gospel and preached by Joachim of Fiore and by yourself? Aren't we forgetting the others?

PIER CELESTINE: I will tell you, in all simplicity, what I think. Can there be any contradiction between a truly Christian soul and the expectation of the Kingdom of God? I don't think so. It seems to me that the Christian soul, which aspires intensely to the Kingdom of God, is formed in the Kingdom's image and bases its behaviour on it, especially all relations with one's fellow-men. It isn't just word-play, to say that the soul achieves, even to a slight degree, the Kingdom. No doubt the conflict between the soul and established institutions and laws goes on. When and how will the Kingdom be set up with the free participation of all creatures? When and how will charity take the place of laws? No one can know that, but we mustn't let this encourage laziness in us. Because the Christians, today and in the future, who live courageously according to that spirit, in reality are anticipating the Kingdom. And in our daily prayer the invocation remains: Thy Kingdom come.

[*Gioacchino and Fra Clementino are visibly convinced, and unable to express their conviction in words, they nod their heads repeatedly.*]

PIER CELESTINE: Before we part, I would like to recommend two further things to you. (*Pause.*) Don't allow your heart to be poisoned by hatred towards the false Christians who persecute us. Those unfortunates who make a commerce of Christ deserve only our pity. Despite the gold they are storing up, they are poor men who must be commiserated. Despite the weapons, the servants in livery, the silken clothing, the Pharaonic ceremonies that surround them, those who find pleasure in such things are ignorant, and the others are wretches. (*Pause.*) As for your own separation from the vain things of this world, since I know you, I know I needn't insist on that. But try not to suffer at the privation. Is the cleanliness of the body a penance? Why should having clean thoughts and clean feelings be a penance then? Be happy.

[*A ragged man appears at the edge of the chasm. Fra Bartolomeo goes towards him at once.*]

FRA BARTOLOMEO (*to the stranger*): Who are you? What are you looking for?
STRANGER (*in a whining voice*): Charity, for the love of God. I haven't eaten for three days.
FRA BARTOLOMEO: Why are you seeking alms in the mountains?
STRANGER (*stammering, barely comprehensible*): I'm a pilgrim . . . I've lost my way . . .

[*Fra Angelo comes over and gives him a piece of bread, motioning him to be off.*]

THE FAITHFUL IN PRISON

A large general cell in the prison of Sulmona. It is a lurid, smoke-blackened room, the walls decorated with obscene scrawlings. A little light comes from two barred windows. Some rings, set in the lower part of the walls, are used to chain up prisoners during the night; in one corner there are a couple of benches. A little iron door opens, the gendarme pushes into the room, one by one—giving the slower ones brutal shoves—the first group of prisoners arrested as accomplices in the flight of the ex-pope Celestine. They are people we already know: Matteo the weaver of Pratola, Fra Ludovico da Macerata, Fra Bartolomeo da Trasacco, Fra Angelo da Caramanico, Fra Berardo da Penne, Fra Tommaso da Atri, and finally three young people: Fra Clementino da Atri and the two Neapolitan ex-clerks, now Celestine novices. These three form a little group on their own, constantly laughing and joking. The prisoners, except for the three young men, are all in bad shape, tired, dusty, dishevelled.

GENDARME: It looks as if, for the present, you're all here. Stay here and keep absolutely silent.
FRA LUDOVICO: Is it permitted . . . to pray?

[*The gendarme doesn't answer.*]

FRA BARTOLOMEO: Can you explain to us why we've been brought in here? Who's coming?

GENDARME: A messenger from the bishop, a theologian and inquisitor of the ecclesiastical court.

FRA ANGELO: Will we remain bound in his presence?

GENDARME: I don't know. It's not for me to decide.

FRA ANGELO: Mind you, I didn't ask because I want to shake the Monsignor's hand.

MATTEO: May we have some water to wash with?

GENDARME: I must remind you this is not an inn, it's a prison.

[*The gendarme goes off, locking the iron door. Once they are alone, the prisoners, who are normally locked in separate cells and are now together for the first time after their arrest, inquire about one another's condition. Fra Bartolomeo introduces to those who don't know them the two Neapolitan ex-clerks, now dressed in secular clothing.*]

FRA BARTOLOMEO: These are two of our novices, who have taken the names of Gioacchino and Luca. As long as our persecution continues, Pier Celestine has authorized them not to wear the habit.

[*Fra Ludovico murmurs something to Fra Clementino, who stands in the centre of the room and holds up his arms for silence.*]

FRA CLEMENTINO: Those who know it by heart are asked to sing with me the first part of the 143rd Psalm, which David wrote when he had hidden in a cavern of the mountains of Judah to escape the persecutions of Saul:
Hear my prayer, O Lord,
Give ear to my supplications:
in thy faithfulness answer me, and in thy righteousness.
    And enter not into judgement with thy servant,
    for in thy sight shall no man living be justified.
    For the enemy hath persecuted my soul;
    he hath smitten my life down to the ground;

he hath made me to dwell in darkness, as those that have
been long dead.
   Therefore is my spirit overwhelmed within me;
   my heart within me is desolate.
I remember the days of old;
I meditate on all thy works;
I muse on the work of thy hands.
   I stretch forth my hands unto thee,
   My soul thirsteth after thee, as a thirsty land . . .

[*When the chanting is over, the older monks sit on the
benches, while the three younger men step forward towards the
footlights, to converse among themselves.*]

FRA CLEMENTINO (*to the two novices*): Is this the first time you've
   been in prison? You must be rather upset.
LUCA: Yes, it's the first time, and I find it less terrible than I
   imagined.
FRA CLEMENTINO: If your soul is at peace and without remorse,
   prison can even be a pleasant place for a rest. Fear of prison
   is a trick invented by the authorities to demoralize good
   Christians. Many acts of cowardice, in fact, are excused by
   the fear of ending in prison.
GIOACCHINO (*to Fra Clementino, with irrepressible anxiety*): Do
   you think our families will be informed of our arrest? I
   admit I'm alarmed about the way my mother might react.
LUCA (*hastens to intervene, to prevent Fra Clementino from saying
   the wrong thing*): You probably don't know that his mother
   is a lady-in-waiting at court. The minute she's told, she'll
   surely run to the king.
FRA CLEMENTINO (*to Gioacchino, laughing*): I was saying you
   shouldn't be afraid of prison; but now I must add that a
   prisoner shouldn't be afraid of being set free either.
GIOACCHINO: What could I do if they set me free by myself?
   Without the rest of you, I'd be like a fish out of water.
FRA CLEMENTINO: You won't be alone, don't worry. Taking the
   proper precautions, you could ask advice of Celestine himself.

GIOACCHINO: Would I be able to find him, without putting him in danger?

FRA CLEMENTINO: It's not easy, but it's possible. You already know Concetta, Matteo's daughter. She's a Christian girl of extraordinary courage and virtue. You can take her news of her father, and if she asks, my news as well. And she will be happy to help you.

[*At this point the conversation among the older monks seated on the bench becomes more lively and attracts the attention of the others. The young people join the larger group.*]

FRA LUDOVICO (*to Fra Angelo, with his voice somewhat raised, since the two of them are seated at opposite ends of the benches*): Fra Angelo, have you heard the latest news of Boniface? He's decreed the annulment of the last donations and privileges given by Pope Celestine to his own monasteries and has deposed a number of bishops named by Celestine in Southern Italy.

FRA BARTOLOMEO: They were formally named by him, but in reality they were appointed by that swindler, the Chancellor Mastrocoeli.

FRA ANGELO: You want to know what I think of it? So much the worse for them, for the monasteries and for the deposed bishops. Compared with the fate of Pier Celestine, nothing is of importance now to my eyes.

FRA LUDOVICO: You're right. When you think about it, what an unlucky man. Like Job, he seems the object of a wager between Satan and God. Just when he had deceived himself that he had recovered his freedom, he lost what little remained to him. We mustn't deceive ourselves either. There will be no more freedom, no more peace, no more repose for our Pier Celestine. Even if he abdicated to return to the hermit's life and even if nothing and no one could make him change his mind, he won't ever live that life. Even if he refuses indignantly to become an instrument of the French, who, for reasons of their own, are determined not to recognize the abdication and persist in considering him the true pope, Celestine won't enjoy that peace. And even if he won't agree to become a tool of Boniface, whose policy he hates and who would like to have him at hand chiefly to snatch him from the French and the Colonnas, Celestine won't have peace. Despite his renunciation and his obstinacy, both sides will go on hunting for him, convinced they can exploit him, with kindness or with force, if they manage to carry him off to Lyons or to Anagni.

FRA TOMMASO: It seems a trap invented by a madman.

FRA BERARDO: No, it's obviously a machination of the devil. Unfortunately for us, a pope is involved.

FRA ANGELO: I thought Boniface was driven only by the fear of being declared anti-pope by the French bishops, who in the end would win the support of the other bishops. But now it's clear he's also filled with envy, or rather with insane hatred of a good Christian. This second motive was revealed to me, openly, by the chamberlain who came here the other day with the abbot of Montecassino. He told me in confidence that, before coming away from Rome, he had left Boniface well disposed towards Pier Celestine; the new pope had spoken about his predecessor with admiration and affection, almost with tenderness. But, later, reports of the public welcome Pier Celestine received on his return to the Abruzzo and the miraculous cures which took place in his presence along the stages of his journey aroused Boniface's suspicions and exasperated him completely. The last instructions, received here by the chamberlain, who—to tell the truth—didn't seem very pleased with them, allowed no room for doubt. Pier Celestine must be captured at all costs and taken to Anagni, in the dead of night and with an armed escort.

LUCA: How can someone be forced to something which his soul refuses?

FRA LUDOVICO: Oh, holy innocence! You don't know the very word "soul" brings a smile to the lips of a man who thinks only of power.

FRA ANGELO: That's so. Boniface or the King of France would need only Celestine's name at their disposal—and also his body, which they could display from time to time, so the people wouldn't believe he was held by force. For the rest, either one of them would leave Celestine free to think as he likes.

GIOACCHINO: What a cruel jest of fate. The Christian who has set aside the crown, rather than use others as objects, now is treated as an object himself. Is there no way out?

FRA LUDOVICO: Celestine fell—with us pushing him—into the machinery of power and that was fatal. Fortunately he became aware of the danger immediately and withdrew in time, before the machinery crushed him. But it's as if the hem of his habit had remained caught in it. It's a cursed machine.

MATTEO: And also, his abdication itself has now made him too important a person to be forgotten in a hermitage. He isn't a private citizen any longer.

GIOACCHINO (*points to the little windows, almost shouting*): Snow! Snow! (*As a Neapolitan, he isn't used to it, so there is a joyous tone to his announcement.*)

LUCA (*to his friend, in a whisper*): Don't forget: for those hiding in the mountains, snow isn't so amusing.

GIOACCHINO (*blanches*): I'm truly a fool.

[*The others also come to the windows. The Morrone is already completely white, and a strong westerly wind is scattering snow over the city. The daylight has turned leaden.*]

MATTEO: This year the snow has come late. People thought it was out of consideration for Pier Celestine, just back from Naples. But, sooner or later, it had to fall. We're in January already.

GIOACCHINO (*timidly*): Do you think the snow means he's in greater danger?

FRA BARTOLOMEO: No, this isn't the first winter he's spent in the mountains.

MATTEO: The first winter as a fugitive, however.

FRA BARTOLOMEO: The snow will cause greater trouble for those who are hunting him. The police, for the most part, are Neapolitans.

MATTEO: But, with the snow, it'll be harder for him to move about when necessary.

FRA BARTOLOMEO: He won't have to move.

MATTEO: Not even if he feels he's in danger?

FRA BARTOLOMEO: Especially if he feels he's in danger.

FRA ANGELO: His nerves are sound, and a period of hibernation will do him good.

FRA LUDOVICO: If he fell ill or had some physical ailment, is there someone who can tend him?

FRA BARTOLOMEO: Yes, he's not alone.

MATTEO: The winter is long on the Morrone. I wonder when we'll see him again.

FRA LUDOVICO: Our imprisonment may be long, too. We must be prepared for a period of hibernation ourselves.

MATTEO: Idleness will be hard for me to bear. I'd prefer forced labour.

[*A key creaks in the lock of the door.*]

FRA BARTOLOMEO: If we are questioned, I propose Fra Angelo answer for all of us.

FRA LUDOVICO: Agreed.

[*The gendarme comes into the room with the bailiff, whom we have seen before.*]

GENDARME: What are you doing by the windows? Line up against that wall.

[*The prisoners obey, the three young men with stiff, military movements.*]

BAILIFF: Someone else was supposed to come and question you, a theologian inquisitor, from here or from Chieti, from the bishopric, I don't really know. We've waited until now for him, but he hasn't appeared. He may arrive any moment.

FRA ANGELO: Unless he's lost his voice, too. (*Laughter.*) Explain

something to us in the meanwhile: under whose juris-
diction have we been imprisoned? The civil court or the
ecclesiastical?

BAILIFF: The question is legitimate, I admit, but at the present
stage of the investigation, it's premature. For the moment
you are held at the disposal of both courts, according to the
agreement stipulated between His Majesty the King of
Naples and His Holiness Boniface VIII. His Majesty has
issued an edict which the town-criers have already published in all the kingdom and which you know. The reason
for your arrest is explained in it. In other words, you can be
set free at once, as soon as you tell us where the ex-pope
Celestine is. (*Prolonged silence.*) You can't pretend you
don't know, because several of you were seen with him just
yesterday morning, in the vicinity of the hermitage of
Sant'Onofrio.

FRA ANGELO: Seen by whom? An honest judge always reveals
the source of his accusation.

BAILIFF: Not in political trials. But because of the respect I feel
towards you, I can take a declaration of yours into account.
Are you prepared to swear you don't know where the
ex-pope is hiding?

FRA ANGELO: The Gospel forbids us to swear.

BAILIFF: I'll forgo the formality of an oath. Are you prepared to
assert as much on your honour?

FRA ANGELO: We have no obligation of honour towards the State
you represent.

BAILIFF: Is there any one among you (*the bailiff looks at each
prisoner individually*) willing to answer this question:
Where is the ex-pope Celestine at present? (*Prolonged
silence.*) Is there anyone who would prefer to speak to me
in private? (*Silence.*) Your silence confirms your guilt, it
seems to me.

FRA ANGELO: No Christian can be forced, in conscience, to
assist the action of his persecutors. Even Our Lord, when
He was in danger of being stoned, concealed Himself.

BAILIFF: Have you received an appeal to revolt against Boniface

VIII, fomented by Pietro and Giacomo Colonna and by your friend Jacopone da Todi? (*Silence.*) I must warn you that, according to the still unpredictable developments of this revolt, you run serious risks if you don't dissociate yourself from it in time.

FRA ANGELO: We are not afraid of those who have the power to harm our body, but of those who destroy the soul.

BAILIFF: Those are fine words that may interest the bishopric's messenger, but not me. (*To the gendarme.*) Would you go and see if he has arrived in the meanwhile? (*The gendarme goes out, and the bailiff continues in a kindly, sorrowing tone of voice.*) I assure you this meeting is painful for me. Unfortunately, in this situation I'm unable to express my deep devotion for Pier Celestine.

FRA ANGELO: Why not? This would be the ideal situation, on the contrary.

FRA BARTOLOMEO: Two months ago you wrote him in Naples, asking him to obtain your promotion from the king.

BAILIFF (*after a moment's hesitation, smiling*): That's possible, quite possible, in view of the times. I think that, in simple common sense, it shouldn't be difficult for our Pier Celestine to choose between the two who are now hunting for him, Pope Boniface, his old friend on the one hand, and the king of France on the other.

FRA ANGELO: There is yet another bully who is seeking him and wants him all for himself.

BAILIFF: I don't know about him. Who might that be?

FRA ANGELO: I think, as a child, even you must have heard his name mentioned: the Lord God.

BAILIFF: Well, that might be another interesting point to be cleared up between you and the bishopric's theologian, but it leaves me absolutely indifferent. I was thinking, on the contrary, that it shouldn't cost our Pier Celestine a great effort to assure his successor of the definitive nature of his abdication and of his refusal to encourage the schism the French are threatening.

FRA ANGELO: You are kicking in an open door, Lord Bailiff.

What you suggest, Pier Celestine has already done, and at first Boniface seemed satisfied. Now he isn't; now he wants the body, dead or alive.

BAILIFF: His suspicions have been aroused, according to the chamberlain, by the public demonstrations and the miracles he worked as he was returning from Naples. It would have been wiser for him to abstain from them.

FRA ANGELO: Miracles, as a pope should know, are worked only by the Lord. If the Most High, when He chooses, makes use of Pier Celestine as intermediary rather than of Boniface, it's obvious that He also assumes the responsibility. Boniface should know therefore where to address his complaints.

BAILIFF: I think this is another matter for the theologian, not for me. (*He breaks off at the sound of the key in the lock, which precedes the reappearance of the gendarme.*)

GENDARME: Somebody has come from the bishopric to say that the theologian inquisitor has a sore throat. (*Laughter, in which even the bailiff joins, to the visible scandal of the gendarme.*)

BAILIFF (*to the prisoners*): Your further stay in prison will depend now on the ecclesiastical court. (*To the gendarme.*) Take the prisoners back to their cells and have them supplied with water for their ablutions.

[*As the gendarme goes to open the door for them again, the bailiff takes Fra Bartolomeo to one side.*]

BAILIFF (*in a low voice*): Your meeting on the Morrone yesterday morning was observed by a false beggar to whom, for that matter, you gave alms. If you can, warn Pier Celestine. Watch out for false beggars. If there's any news, I'll come to you in your cell.

[*Darkness.*]

V

Vieste (Gargano). May, 1295

*The action takes place at Vieste, on the Southern coast of the
Gargano, an inaccessible place which can be reached only by boat.
The scene depicts a broad, shallow cavern half-way up a rocky
promontory, almost projecting over the sea. Around the cave there
are some clumps of prickly-pear and a few wild olives; a path, in
front of it, widens into a kind of little terrace. Some huge rocks
serve as places to sit.*

*It is a calm afternoon in the month of May, 1295. Six months
have gone by since Pope Celestine's abdication and the beginning of
his flight from the agents of Boniface the VIII and his French
rivals. Pier Celestine is resting now inside the cave, which is
illuminated by the setting sun; he is seated on a straw pallet, his
back and head against the rock, his eyes closed. Gioacchino
observes him, uncertain whether or not to waken him, to announce
the arrival of Clementino. He decides against it. The two young
people, for reasons of prudence, now wear secular clothing. The
newcomer is seated on the ground in front of the cave.*

CLEMENTINO (*nodding towards Pier Celestine*): Is he asleep?

GIOACCHINO: Yes. Some sleep would do you good, too. How
   long did it take you to reach here?

CLEMENTINO: Four days. I'm tired now, but not sleepy. We have
   many things to tell each other.

GIOACCHINO: Many things. (*Overcoming evident hesitation.*) Will
   Concetta be coming soon, too?

CLEMENTINO: I think so. If it depended on her alone, she
   would already be here; but she's travelling with her father,
   and he has to move more slowly, because of his age.

GIOACCHINO: Concetta's a remarkable girl. While we were in
   prison, she hid the refugees and fed them.

CLEMENTINO: Yes, she's marvellous in every way. Was she the one who led you to Pier Celestine?

GIOACCHINO: It was an experience I'll never forget. I'll probably talk to you about it many times in the future, but now I want to tell you the essential part, also because it concerns Pier Celestine. She and I set out at evening to elude the surveillance of the police spies, and night soon overtook us. Luckily the sky was clear and there was a moon. But gradually, as we advanced, the snow became deeper, and in some places we sank into it up to our waists. She went ahead and so it was harder for her; I followed her, climbing in her tracks. Several times I suggested we change places, but she refused. "You don't know the road," she would answer. I can't tell you how cold it was, or how afraid I was of wolves; it was only pride that kept me on my feet, yes, a man's pride in the company of a girl. Alone, or with another man, with you for example, I wouldn't have made it; I would have collapsed totally. After several hours of that horrible Calvary, in the heart of the night, we could make out Pier Celestine's secret refuge, thank God. Concetta said: "You see that dark rock up there?" I told her I could see it. "Fine," she said, "Good night and God bless you," and she turned her back to go down again. As soon as I recovered from my surprise, with what little energy I had left, I started shouting: "Concetta, Concetta." She turned towards me: "What's wrong?" she asked. "You can't go back down that path again, at this hour, alone, without any rest, it's madness," I shouted. "Pier Celestine will punish me if I allow you to do it." "If that's what's worrying you," she answered, "you can be sure he won't reproach you," and she resumed her mad race towards the valley. Naturally I wasn't worried about anyone's reproaches; I had mentioned Pier Celestine just because I myself felt that if I let her go, I would deserve punishment. But I was so exhausted I couldn't do anything. So I stood there in a daze looking towards the valley, even for a long time after she had vanished into the mist.

CLEMENTINO: Did you talk about her with Pier Celestine?

GIOACCHINO: Immediately, as soon as I was in his presence. But first I must tell you that when, with great suffering, I managed to drag myself to the vicinity of the refuge, I was attacked by two huge, fierce dogs that were standing guard. They were two of those terrible Abruzzese mastiffs, with white fur; men clip their ears to sharpen their hearing and put iron collars on them, bristling with nails, to defend them against wolves in the night. Those horrible animals flung themselves on me and in a few moments they had reduced me to a sorry state. They would easily have killed me, if some shepherds hadn't quickly rushed from the refuge to help me. They carried me inside in their arms. I had deep, bleeding wounds in various places and my clothes were in tatters. The dogs' bites might even have given me rabies. But I had no time to think about that; my only concern obviously was Concetta and, precisely because of her, I was immediately seized with a violent access of anger at Pier Celestine, as I will explain to you. The first words I managed to stammer out were to tell him how much strength and courage the girl had shown in accompanying me to within a short distance of him, and then, without my being able to prevent it, how she had gone back, running grave risks which could easily be imagined. I begged Pier Celestine to send one of those shepherds to overtake her at once, to persuade her to spend the night with us, or else to see her safely home. When I thought I had made myself clear, I waited tensely—I could even say with anguish—for his decision; but he remained silent. Then I suspected that, because of his age, he hadn't heard my words, and that he had even fallen asleep. In fact, the cave was dimly lighted by a couple of oil lanterns and I couldn't make out his features clearly. I was in despair. I didn't know what to do. Though I was prostrated by my journey and the pain of my wounds, I began again, breathlessly, telling my story in a louder voice, shaking his arm to waken him, if that was necessary. But he interrupted me brusquely, and with a harshness I didn't believe him capable of: "I understand," he shouted, "I understand. Now be silent." He didn't add another word, not a thing about Concetta. At that moment I began to hate him.

CLEMENTINO: I understand you. In the state of mind you were in, it was the most natural reaction. Only, when you could think more coolly, you might have imagined Celestine had a reason for his behaviour, a reason you didn't know and which, for that matter, I wouldn't be able to guess even now.

GIOACCHINO: I admire your wisdom, but I was far from being so wise. If I had been able to get up the following morning and stand on my feet, I would have gone away, had nothing further to do with him. But the next day, they told me later, I was delirious, with a high fever, and so fortunately I was obliged to stay. I repeat, fortunately, because I was able to know Celestine better and love him once again.

[*At this point the two young men notice that Pier Celestine is awake and is listening to them. Clementino hastens to stand up and kiss his hand.*]

CLEMENTINO (*to Pier Celestine*): When I arrived you were resting and I didn't want to disturb you.

[*Pier Celestine also takes a seat at the entrance of the cave, beside Gioacchino and Clementino.*]

PIER CELESTINE: Please forgive me for my bad manners. As soon as I woke and noticed Clementino's presence, I was about to welcome him, but then I heard you were speaking ill of me, and I gave way to the pleasure of listening to you. Now it's no use my begging Gioacchino to continue as if I were asleep, because it would only be a pretence.

CLEMENTINO: Still I'm eager to know how the two of you arrived at a reconciliation.

PIER CELESTINE (*to Clementino*): It was up to me to make the first move, since—at least apparently—I was in the wrong. As soon as Gioacchino was conscious and able to take things in, at a moment when we were alone, I said to him: "If, the other evening, I had agreed to your suggestion and had made one of these gentlemen run after Concetta, I tell you I would have exposed her to a far greater risk than any encounter with a wolf. You didn't know the social position of our hosts here, and I couldn't explain it to you in their presence."

CLEMENTINO: Social position?

GIOACCHINO (*to Clementino, with childish exaggeration*): In other words, they were—they still are—bandits. You understand? Real bandits, the kind Abruzzese wet-nurses tell tales about and make children have worms out of fear.

PIER CELESTINE: They are a band I had heard the shepherds talk about several times in the past; they told frightening stories of the so-called Band of the Billhook. They are charged with a long list of crimes of every sort, but at present the band devotes its time preferably to stealing livestock.

CLEMENTINO: I don't understand their interest in an ex-pope with no flocks or herds. How did you fall into their keeping?

PIER CELESTINE (*visibly annoyed by all this story*): They arrived at Sant'Onofrio just before the police, and Fra Bartolomeo recognized one of them as an honest shepherd of the Morrone. As it turned out, he was a formerly honest shepherd.

CLEMENTINO: But I still can't understand why they took you under their wing.

GIOACCHINO (*to Pier Celestine*): May I answer?

PIER CELESTINE: Yes, but be brief. Those rogues have already wasted too much of my time.

GIOACCHINO: I discussed it once or twice with the leader of the band, a sly, brutal man. "Why does Pier Celestine interest you?" I asked him. He was seriously offended that I dare question his selflessness. "He's one of us," the man kept saying, "one of our mountain, he's our flesh and blood; before they arrest him, they'll have to pass over our dead bodies." He seemed sincere to me. On the other hand, they used Pier Celestine as bait to carry out some very profitable raids against the police. (*To Pier Celestine*.) You should tell Clementino how they seized all the horses of a squadron of gendarmes sent to search for you.

PIER CELESTINE: Frankly, I don't want to. You can tell Clementino those scoundrels' exploits on some other occasion. Now I'm eager for him to tell us the latest news of our friends.

CLEMENTINO: I delayed telling the news because it's sad. Have you heard about Fra Angelo da Caramanico?

PIER CELESTINE: Where is he?

CLEMENTINO: He was with us in the prison in Sulmona. But when he answered too vigorously the questioning of a theologian from the bishopric, he was sent to the prison at Bolsena which, as you know, is reserved for ecclesiastics. A short time afterwards, no one knows how, he died there.

PIER CELESTINE (*sadly afflicted by this news*): Oh infamy, oh wickedness without a name, oh unspeakable evil: to strike down a man so pure, honest, good. (*Covers his face with his hands*.) Poor Pope Boniface, we must pray God to forgive him.

CLEMENTINO: In the Marches there have been cases of friars scourged in the streets. Many other friends of ours are wandering in the mountains and we have no news of them. Fra Liberato, Fra Clareno, and Fra Ludovico, however, have safely escaped to Greece.

PIER CELESTINE: And while this was happening to my sons and brothers, I was stupidly idle in the hands of criminals.

CLEMENTINO: Couldn't you leave them?

PIER CELESTINE: They wouldn't let us.

GIOACCHINO: I tried in vain to persuade the chief. "It would be a dishonour for us," he answered, "the law of hospitality is the first commandment of the mountains; Celestine is the pride of our land," and things of that sort.

PIER CELESTINE: When they resigned themselves to allowing me to leave, it was practically impossible.

GIOACCHINO: Snow storms had blocked all the passes. Any trace of a path had vanished. Wolves were sighted almost every day. Finally we came to a compromise: we would be left free in May. Not before, since they were expecting more horses to come by in April.

PIER CELESTINE: The prior of San Giovanni in Piano has now placed a boat with a couple of fishermen at our disposal, to take us to Greece. On Achaia in the gulf of Corinth, we'll find our friends who went ahead of us. We're waiting for the wind to shift, then we'll leave. Our Fra Tommaso da Sulmona is down below with the fishermen, taking care of the other practical questions.

CLEMENTINO: So you too have decided to go into exile, to safety? I'm happy. Here you're in permanent danger.

PIER CELESTINE: Yes, I had always refused to leave: you're right to remind me of that. Exile is sad, I said, it's a form of confessing one's own defeat and leaving the field to the adversary. But what can I do here now? My sons and brothers are scattered. (*His eyes turned to heaven.*) And yet, my God, I didn't ask much, only to be left in peace with some of them. You saw fit not to grant me this. Now the only freedom left me is a choice of slavery: with Boniface, with the King of France, or with a band of cattle thieves. For various reasons I can't accept any of them. (*The two young men listen, moved and silent, to the Father's lament.*) My sons, look at this land, these stones, the sea, the sky: fill your soul with these sights, that you may think of them again when you are far away. You must love your own land, but if it becomes uninhabitable for those who want to retain their personal dignity, then it's best to go away. Our justification isn't contemptible since it isn't prompted by laziness, but by the mission before us.

[*From the right Fra Tommaso da Sulmona appears.*]

FRA TOMMASO (*to Pier Celestine*): Father, the fishermen tell me the wind is finally in our favour. If you like, we can leave.

PIER CELESTINE: Very well, at once. (*To Fra Tommaso and to Clementino.*) You two don't know each other? This is an old companion, Fra Tommaso da Sulmona, and this is Fra Clementino da Atri, now in secular clothing.

GIOACCHINO (*after exchanging meaningful glances with Fra Clementino*): Couldn't we wait until tomorrow?

CLEMENTINO: If that's possible, it would be better.

PIER CELESTINE (*surprised*): Why? Do you regret your decision?

GIOACCHINO and CLEMENTINO: No, no, not at all.

PIER CELESTINE: Then why delay, if the wind is favourable to us at last? That was all we were waiting for.

GIOACCHINO: This evening or tomorrow morning Matteo and Concetta might arrive.

CLEMENTINO: We'd like to say goodbye to them before leaving. We don't know how long it will be before we see one another again, if we ever will.

PIER CELESTINE: I understand you. I'll go and tell Fra Tommaso. Concetta deserves this.

GIOACCHINO (*exultant*): I'm happy to hear you say so.

PIER CELESTINE: Are you surprised?

GIOACCHINO: Sincerely, I am.

PIER CELESTINE: Why?

GIOACCHINO: I wouldn't like to reopen a wound that is now healed. But, you remember, that evening of my arrival at the refuge, Concetta refused to follow me, not because of the shepherds, whose bandit activity she knew nothing about, but to avoid incurring your disapproval. Was she mistaken perhaps?

PIER CELESTINE: She wasn't mistaken, although she may also have attributed that opinion to me in order to support her own, natural way of behaving. I don't believe Concetta has ever spent a night away from home, without some member of her family. But this would lead us to other things, and I won't insist, because I don't want to evade your reproach. It affects me, believe me, profoundly. It's true, it's always been hard for me to be casual and courteous with women, as Christ was and as Saint Francis was. I'm not an angel, but a humble Christian with many prejudices, much clumsiness and limitations which make me suffer. To return to Concetta, I've never conversed with her, but what I know of her fills me with admiration.

(*Pause.*) At times I've even thought: a pity that girl isn't a man.

GIOACCHINO (*who has followed Celestine's words with great satisfaction, now becomes indignant at this last remark*): It seems to me she makes a very fine girl. (*To Fra Clementino.*) What do you think?

CLEMENTINO: Yes, I agree, Concetta makes a fine girl.

PIER CELESTINE: I expressed myself badly. What I meant was that, with her excellent qualities, she could have achieved a proper position if she were a man.

GIOACCHINO: A position in what sense? In the sense of a career? No, you don't think that. In what sense then? I feel that everything she does is very well done, and she couldn't do it any better even if she were a man. (*To Clementino.*) What do you think?

CLEMENTINO: I feel that everything she does is done very well.

PIER CELESTINE (*laughing*): I see I'm in the minority, so I will be silent.

[*The monk seen before now reappears.*]

FRA TOMMASO: I don't like to insist, but it's best to hurry. At Peschici, not far from here, there is murmuring about you. One of the fishermen, who has just come from there, was questioned by a gendarme.

PIER CELESTINE (*dismissing further delay*): It's best to avoid the risk; we'll leave at once. (*To Gioacchino.*) In the boat we'll say an Ave Maria and think of Concetta. Do you believe in the communion of souls?

GIOACCHINO: Of course. Concetta believes in it, too.

PIER CELESTINE: You've spoken with her about it.

GIOACCHINO: Yes, and for that reason the separation will be less sad. She said to me: how would it be possible to bear loneliness without faith in the communion of souls?

PIER CELESTINE (*admiringly*): Is that what she said? She is really an extraordinary girl . . . Too bad she's not a man. Oh, I'm sorry, I take back those last words.

[*Darkness.*]

THE USELESS FLIGHT

*Light. The action resumes in the same setting as the preceding
scene. A month later. Various details indicate the cave is inhabited
and that time has gone by since the previous scene: summer has
followed spring. On the path that winds up from the shore Matteo
the weaver appears. He is wearing a tunic which hangs almost to
his knees, a cowl on his head. He seems aged, tired, dejected; he is
laboriously dragging a heavy sack after him. When he comes to
the cave, he glances inside, sees no one, then sits on the sack to
catch his breath and mop the copious sweat from his face. After a
moment he calls his daughter, who is late in overtaking him.*

MATTEO: Concetta?

CONCETTA (*not yet visible*): I'm coming. I'll be right there.

> [*The girl is wearing a little cloak about her shoulders, and on
> her head, protected by a round pad, she carries a heavy
> bundle, wrapped in a hempen sheet, which she sets at a side of
> the cave. Despite the trials of the journey, she remains fresh
> and youthful.*]

MATTEO: Our home will be like this, too. (*Shudders with horror.*)
Caves were specially made to encourage rheumatism.

CONCETTA: Before winter comes we'll look for something
better.

MATTEO: Did you find anyone in the hut on the rocks?

CONCETTA: Our boatman's mother. She told me what her son
had said. The Saint—that's what she calls Pier Celestine—
was barely saved from a shipwreck. It was a real miracle,
she says, and the next day he left these parts. She couldn't,
or wouldn't tell me where he went. The two young men
who were with him stayed here.

MATTEO: Where are they? I don't see them.

CONCETTA: The old woman went to tell them. She said that at
first they expected us any day, but in the end they lost all
hope of seeing us arrive.

MATTEO (*complains again*): I don't think I'll get used to this place. Everything is hostile here, the mountain, the vegetation, the sea. On the boat I thought I was going to drown at any moment.

CONCETTA: It seemed terrible to you because we're not used to it. But didn't you hear how the boatman sang? That means there was no danger.

MATTEO (*racked with shudders from time to time*): All that water. Good God, I never imagined so much water could exist. What's the use of so much water? And then this gypsy life is not for me.

CONCETTA: It's not for me either and I also hope our wandering will soon end. Remember what the prior of San Giovanni in Piano promised us. He wants to help us set up a loom around here. He said we would have many orders immediately.

MATTEO: I haven't forgotten. But you know how hard it is to start from the beginning in our craft? And once the work is under way, will we be left in peace? Won't we have to flee again, like criminals?

CONCETTA: Father, how can I answer you? Let's hope not.

[*The girl goes into the cave and begins to put it in order, as if it were her own home. In one corner she finds a bundle of dirty clothes which she gathers on a plank, preparing to go and wash them.*]

MATTEO (*resumes his complaints*): We came here because we were called by Pier Celestine. If he's gone, what are we doing here?

CONCETTA: Maybe he's nearby. Maybe he left some word for us. The friars will tell us. Just be patient for a little longer. Anyway, you know you can't go back to Sulmona, the baron has forbidden us to use the stream and the authorities have banished you.

MATTEO: You can't sit still for a minute. Where are you going now with those clothes?

CONCETTA: I'm going to wash them. The boatman's mother

told me about a spring near here, where they also do the washing.

[*But suddenly shouts of joy are heard from the path and a moment later Gioacchino and Clementino run up. The encounter is very affectionate, with long and repeated hand-clasps and cries of "at last, at last, how are you, it's been so long".*]

GIOACCHINO: To tell the truth, we had given you up.

CONCETTA (*pretending to scold*): Man of little faith.

MATTEO: It's my fault we're so late. I wasn't well, or rather, I was very ill.

CONCETTA: Where is Pier Celestine now?

[*The question embarrasses the two young men.*]

GIOACCHINO: We have all sorts of news to tell you. But where shall we begin?

CONCETTA: We've heard about the shipwreck. You had set out for Greece and the sea drove you back. And then?

GIOACCHINO: When we came back, we were told that at Peschici, nearby, an expedition had arrived to capture Pier Celestine.

CLEMENTINO: We should add that his slightest movement was followed and checked. It was hard for him to hide. Still the local authorities didn't dare lay hands on him, for fear of arousing the wrath of the faithful.

GIOACCHINO: In the end, however, a captain of the sheep levy informed his superiors that Pier Celestine had taken refuge here, in the Gargano. The report reached the king who, to tell the truth, avoided giving the capture any odious aspect. He assigned the task to a prelate with the title of Patriarch of Jerusalem and to various gentlemen with their families. The delegation was to present itself to Pier Celestine as if to pay him homage. But he refused this pretence and gave himself up as a prisoner.

CONCETTA: Why didn't he escape? Why didn't you resist his surrender?

CLEMENTINO: We argued a great deal with him. But there was no way of convincing him to flee again, although our friends here insisted it would be very easy. Perhaps he felt he was a burden to us. Perhaps he thought that, without him, we would act more freely.

GIOACCHINO: He said to us: "In a little while the worms will have my carcass; what is the harm if, before the worms, Boniface's jailers have it? Naturally," he added, "just the carcass, and nothing else." He agreed to be accompanied only by Fra Tommaso da Sulmona, whom you probably know.

CONCETTA: So you allowed him to go out to his jailers.

CLEMENTINO: He who trusts in the Lord is like Mount Zion; nothing can shake him, he is steadfast forever.

GIOACCHINO: As soon as we were alone, we plunged headlong into the task he set for us. Here in the Gargano we're establishing a base for exchanging messages and documents with the exiles who have taken refuge in Greece and with our friends in the various provinces. We're trying to disguise this activity as something above suspicion, ordinary trade. Various boatmen help us. Our Clementino has just come back yesterday from Greece with writings of Clareno and of Fra Ludovico. This evening we'll read you some of them: their spiritual strength is very moving. We've already begun making copies for our friends in the provinces. (*To Concetta.*) For delivering them to their destination we're counting on you, too, and on those girls, your friends in Sulmona. You could make use of the next big pilgrimages. We'll discuss ways. I must tell you that Pier Celestine, when he was giving us these instructions, mentioned your help several times.

CLEMENTINO: Shall we tell Concetta with what trust and esteem Pier Celestine spoke of her?

CONCETTA (*blushing*): But he hardly knows me! Well, we'll talk about the pilgrimages, but now there are more urgent things. Have you had news of him?

GIOACCHINO: Who would send us news? Boniface?

CONCETTA: If no one brings us the news we want, we can go and
    look for it ourselves, don't you think? Didn't you say that
    Clementino made a special trip to Greece?
MATTEO: Daughter, it's not easy to find out where Pier Celestine
    has been confined or if it's possible to communicate with
    him.
CONCETTA: Where is it written that we must do only easy things?
    Please, forgive me, father, I don't mean to criticize you,
    but for myself, I don't see how it's possible to sleep, not
    knowing if he is still alive or if he's dead and how he died.
    Suppose he needs us?

[*Darkness.*]

VI

Anagni, Palazzo Caetani

BONIFACE VIII AND PIER CELESTINE

A room with an armchair on a dais, surmounted by a canopy: the domestic throne of Boniface VIII. Chairs at either side. Pier Celestine is standing in one corner of the room, wearing his usual hermit's habit. He seems wasted and he leans against the frame of a window, to support himself. Boniface VIII comes in and goes straight to the throne, where he sits down with his natural haughtiness and indifference.

BONIFACE VIII (*after having observed Pier Celestine, as if to recognize him, points to a chair at his own right hand*): You may sit. It seems you've refused to be examined by my physician.

PIER CELESTINE (*bows and sits down*): I am not ill.

BONIFACE VIII: Old age in itself is an illness.

PIER CELESTINE: But the physician for my old age is Our Lord.

BONIFACE VIII: I have also been informed that, since you have been here, you have hardly touched food. Why? Are you afraid of being poisoned?

PIER CELESTINE: My customary nourishment has always been frugal. There are poor people who eat even less, and yet they work from morning to night.

BONIFACE VIII: Are you comfortable in my house? Have you any complaints?

PIER CELESTINE: Oh, no, how could I dare? (*He looks around and then observes the ceiling and adds, without any irony*) The roof doesn't leak.

[*The pope bursts out laughing, then remains silent for a while, observing his "guest". He even seems quite moved by him.*]

BONIFACE VIII: You know, during the first weeks of your pontificate, in Naples, seeing you as you were then and as you are now . . .

PIER CELESTINE (*surprised*): How am I?

BONIFACE VIII: . . . I felt moved towards you by true affection and, I would say, by tenderness. How strange, I said to myself, how strange, a Christian of this sort in our world. In a certain way it seemed a fable, a dream . . .

PIER CELESTINE: I soon opened my eyes and it became a nightmare. I thank you for having helped me leave it.

BONIFACE VIII: If you knew all the nonsense they're saying now about my part in persuading you to abdicate.

PIER CELESTINE: But you are convinced that it was a free act of my own conscience?

BONIFACE VIII: Of course. My modest advice was limited to certain formalities.

PIER CELESTINE (*bitterly*): Then how could you believe, afterwards, that I felt any nostalgia for the pontificate?

BONIFACE VIII (*vigorously*): No, I never imagined such a thing, I assure you. If I was forced to give orders . . . severe orders concerning you, I did so only to protect myself against the misuse others might make of your name and your person, against your own will.

PIER CELESTINE: With the help of God, I know how to protect myself, by myself. (*In a low, firm voice.*) You will realize that.

BONIFACE VIII: Surely you don't mean to consider the pope in the same category with the enemies of the Church?

[*Pier Celestine doesn't answer. The pope resists the impulse to make certain demands at once, and he resigns himself to informing Pier Celestine of his own difficulties.*]

BONIFACE VIII: You come from the solitary life and naturally you don't know about certain serious events that have taken place recently. I feel it's my duty to inform you. I am not referring to the sedition of the Colonnas, which is the least of my worries. But I have received very bad news from Paris and London. A conflict between the Holy See and Edward of England and Philip the Fair is now inevitable. I won't draw back and I shall refuse any compromise. The moment has come, I think, to raise solemnly, before all Christendom and all States, the fundamental question of the principle of authority. Expedients and trafficking must be ended once and for all. The Church of Rome must return to the great vision of Innocent and Gregory. Just look at the condition Europe is in: the great emperors have disappeared. Who sets himself up against us? What authentic power? What idea? Just as Gregory the Great was able to exploit the weakness of the Byzantine Empire...

PIER CELESTINE (*timidly raises his hand*): May I say a word? My concerns, Your Holiness, I must confess to you, are of another nature. I am frightened by the growing secularization of the Church of Christ. She has become unrecognizable.

BONIFACE VIII: Don't you realize that, nowadays, the Church can't withdraw from the political scene and remain inert? What will become of Europe if the Church doesn't intervene courageously? What will happen to Christianity? Before it's too late, the Church must reaffirm, *ex cathedra*, her superiority over all human establishments. Mind you, no theologian casts any doubt on the legitimacy of this position. Christ entrusted to us the "potestas legandi atque solvendi in coelo et in terra": the power to bind and to loosen on earth and in heaven. Saint Paul restated it, in lapidary terms in the Epistle to the Romans: "Omnis potestas a Deo": all power comes from God. If human society is one, how can separate powers be conceivable? The Church, as direct emanation of the divine will, is therefore meant to hold both swords: the spiritual sword, which she holds herself in the priestly hand, and the temporal sword, equally *pro Ecclesia*, which she entrusts to kings and captains worthy of her faith.

PIER CELESTINE: Your Holiness, may I speak without scandalizing you? I don't like swords, of any kind.

BONIFACE VIII: You must nevertheless be aware that they govern the world.

PIER CELESTINE (*humbly and firmly*): Power doesn't attract me, I find it essentially wicked. The Christian commandment which sums up all the others is love. During the past months, while I was hidden to elude your police, I have become more aware than I was in the past that the root of all evils, for the Church, lies in the temptation of power.

BONIFACE VIII: Would you abandon power to our enemies?

PIER CELESTINE: Our kingdom is not of this world. Our kingdom . . .

BONIFACE VIII (*with a gesture of impatience*): I know the prophecies, when I was younger I used to enjoy reading them too. Did the good news of Christ really contain the announcement of the world's imminent end? Some authors insist it did, and so be it. But we are compelled to recognize that the world goes on: isn't that true?

PIER CELESTINE: That doesn't seem to me a good reason for Christianity to renounce its nature and move into the world, as if the world were to last for all eternity.

BONIFACE VIII: What does it matter how long the world lasts? What do I know of that? What can you know of the possible duration of the world? The important thing is to affirm the Church's superiority in it, the only possible reality.

PIER CELESTINE: In adapting itself to the world, what has happened to Christianity? How far has it been corrupted or transformed by the world? We have forgotten that Christianity began on the Cross . . .

BONIFACE VIII: Would you have preferred for it to remain there?

PIER CELESTINE: Let's leave preferences out of this; each of us has his own. But why go on calling ourselves Christians? What has the Cross become for the Christians of today? An ornament, an object. I wonder if we really believe in the same God. Sometimes I doubt it.

BONIFACE VIII: Our faith is Christian; you wouldn't dare deny that.

PIER CELESTINE: Faith cannot be separated from hope and charity. How can we allow the infamous titles of Christian armies, Christian wars, Christian persecutions, and other ignominy of that sort?

BONIFACE VIII: The term Christian is used to mean the end, the intention, the purpose . . .

PIER CELESTINE: You can't kill for a good end. To good ends you can do only good, love, help one another, forgive.

BONIFACE VIII: In short, as I repeat, since you're not in a position to abolish political power, would you turn it over to the enemies of the Church? This is the point. The rest is just talk.

PIER CELESTINE: Are souls just talk?

BONIFACE VIII: I don't like word games.

PIER CELESTINE: I detest them myself. So if we can't convince each other, let's try at least to understand each other. When we talk of the reality that must be taken into consideration, you refer to institutions and to power, I refer to souls. Please correct me, if I'm mistaken.

BONIFACE VIII: Does such a sharp distinction exist? Aren't souls dependent on institutions?

PIER CELESTINE: They can be dependent on them, but the task of Christianity is to redeem through truth. God created souls, not institutions. Souls are immortal, not institutions, not kingdoms, not armies, not churches, not nations. (*The pope, disheartened, makes a gesture, as if giving up any idea of replying; after a brief pause Pier Celestine continues.*) Your Holiness, if you look out of that window, you will see on the steps of the cathedral a ragged old woman, a beggar, a creature of no importance in the life of this world, who sits there from morning to evening. But in a million years, or a thousand million years, her soul will still exist, because God made it immortal. While the kingdom of Naples, of France, of England, all the other kingdoms, with their armies, their tribunals, their fanfares and the rest will have returned to nothingness.

BONIFACE VIII: Your example makes me laugh, Pier Celestine. Mightn't the salvation or damnation of that little soul that means so much to you depend on the assistance that she receives in this world from some charitable institution?

PIER CELESTINE: No, if you'll allow me to contradict you, it depends only on God's mercy. She might be given alms enough to allow her to eke out an existence also by an institution that isn't Christian. Christianity, as you know better than I, is something more than almsgiving. It demands love of charity, love of enemies . . .

BONIFACE VIII: Et cetera, et cetera, we know all that. But why can't you admit that it would be absurd to turn those heroic commandments into a rule of government?

PIER CELESTINE: I agree, Your Holiness, as a rule of government they would be absurd. But if Christianity is stripped of its so-called absurdities to make it more welcome to the world and more suited to the wielding of power, then what is left of it? You know that reasonableness, common sense, natural virtues existed before Christ, and can be found now, too, in many non-Christians. What did Christ bring us beyond them? Some apparent absurdities, in fact. He told us: love poverty, love the meek and the oppressed, love your enemies, give no thought to power, to success, to honours, they are ephemeral things, unworthy of immortal souls . . .

BONIFACE VIII: Enough, please . . . While you were still pope, I couldn't refuse to listen to your country-parson sermons; but now, frankly, I find them unbearable. (*Pause.*) Rather than waste more time, I'll tell you exactly what actions, I, as pope, demand of you. The Church, as I've already explained to you, is about to encounter serious difficulties and she needs the unity of all her sons. Gregory VII did not hesitate to depose Henry IV and I, if necessary, will follow his example. I will not give up the right, granted me by God, to excommunicate, to depose, to damn.

PIER CELESTINE (*his hands joined, in a pleading voice*): Be more meek, Your Holiness, have compassion at least for the many souls that will be exposed to persecution by those monarchs. Our Lord set us an example. Put up your sword, He commanded Peter. If we can't overcome our adversaries with good, how can we think to defeat them with threats?

BONIFACE VIII: I beg you to stop using expressions of this sort, which for me are meaningless. (*Very harshly.*) Answer my questions instead. First of all: are you ready to condemn publicly the opinions and heretical acts of Ubertino da Casale, of Clareno, and the other madmen who follow them?

PIER CELESTINE (*seriously embarrassed*): I have no reason to doubt their good faith. And how could I set myself up as judge of their consciences? Moreover, they are in exile.

BONIFACE VIII (*strikes his fist violently on the arm of his chair*): You dare defend them? Don't you know that in the past few days they have managed to send some of their blasphemous writings to Rome itself?

PIER CELESTINE (*smiling*): All the way to Rome?

BONIFACE VIII: I assure you that, sooner or later, those friends of yours will fall in my hands, and then they will receive the punishment they deserve.

PIER CELESTINE (*reassured*): It might be, Your Holiness, that in the sight of God, in this sad century, the honour of the name of Christian has been entrusted to those poor men.

BONIFACE VIII (*gripped by furious wrath*): You permit yourself, in my house, not only to defend those scoundrels, but to praise them? You don't realize what might happen to you.

PIER CELESTINE (*sadly*): I fear nothing any more, Your Holiness, but I tremble for your soul. To use violence against one's own brothers, in disagreements of a religious nature, is a sacrilege, don't forget that. It's a sin against the Holy Spirit.

BONIFACE VIII (*springs to his feet, shouting*): I command you to be silent. (*A violent attack of asthma makes him pause.*) I have nothing further to ask you and we have nothing further to say to each other. You have thrust away the hand I held out to you and there is no sense in your staying in my house any longer.

PIER CELESTINE (*also standing, shaken with emotion*): I have not been a guest in this house, but a prisoner, as you know. You wish to send me away now? Very well. (*With ill-concealed anxiety.*) Will you restore me to my children?

BONIFACE VIII (*has already come down from the throne and is heading for the door; he turns brusquely towards Pier Celestine*): How dare you hope for that? No, no. You will receive instead the punishment you deserve.

PIER CELESTINE (*makes him a deep bow, resigned, and answers gently*): I will pray for you.

[*Darkness.*]

THE MYSTERY OF THE END

A dimly-lighted street-corner in Anagni. Concetta is seated on a stone outside a doorway and, at her feet, she has a basket with skeins of wool, like a peasant-woman at the market. From time to time, she repeats to the public, in a kind of chant: "Wool, wool, good wool from the Maiella." After a little while Gioacchino arrives, also dressed as a peasant, carrying a knapsack on his back.

GIOACCHINO (*whispering, to Concetta*): I've found that man from your village. He's in a convent.

CONCETTA: Do you have news of him?

GIOACCHINO: I think so.

CONCETTA: He'll tell you right away, he's following me.

[*Old Fra Tommaso da Sulmona limps past the two, without stopping, without even looking at them.*]

CONCETTA (*to Gioacchino, disappointed*): He didn't recognize us.

GIOACCHINO: Oh yes, he did . . . Here he is, coming back.

[*Fra Tommaso returns towards the girl and pretends to be interested in the wool she is selling.*]

CONCETTA: Fra Tommaso, may God bless you.

FRA TOMMASO: Honoured daughter of Matteo, peace be with you.

CONCETTA: We're anxious to know where our Pier Celestine is, how he is, and what we can do for him.

FRA TOMMASO (*holds up a pair of skeins in his hand as if examining them*): He was imprisoned for a little while, here in Anagni, in the palace of the Caetanis near the Cathedral . . .

CONCETTA: We know where it is. We had someone show us as soon as we arrived, and we've been trying to find a way to get inside.

FRA TOMMASO: But he isn't there any more. Boniface kept him in the palace as long as he hoped to obtain something from him. When he became convinced it was hopeless, he flew into a terrible rage and had Pier Celestine taken to the fortress of Fumone.

CONCETTA: Fumone? Is that far from here?

FRA TOMMASO (*looks around suspiciously*): There isn't enough light in this doorway for me to examine this wool of yours. Let's go over there, where I can see it better.

[*With basket and knapsack, the three of them come down towards the footlights.*]

FRA TOMMASO (*after looking around once more*): You see that tower, on that rocky peak? That's Fumone. It's a place with a very sad reputation. The prisoners' cells are no bigger than a grave. The prisoners have to crawl into them, and there are no windows.

CONCETTA: Is there any way to approach the tower?

FRA TOMMASO: You can go as far as Alatri, that big village on the hill, but no higher than that. The fortress is full of armed men.

CONCETTA (*her eyes full of tears, looking at the peak*): Oh, our dear, dear, dear old man. At his age, among hostile, brutal people, treated like a fierce criminal . . . he, of all people, always so good and so kind with everyone . . . What's the use of our love if we can't do anything for him?

GIOACCHINO (*to Fra Tommaso*): Tell me, what will they do with him? What do you think?

FRA TOMMASO (*slowly, hesitantly, almost stammering because of his inner dismay*): It's probable they'll offer him some further compromise. And there's no doubt he will refuse. And then I'm afraid they will kill him . . . And then, then they will make him a saint. We mustn't try to understand. The destiny of some saints, while they're alive, is one of the most profound mysteries of the Church.

[THE END]

NOTES

Joachim of Fiore

He was born at Celico, in the province of Cosenza, around 1130, of a peasant family. After a journey to the Holy Land, he entered the Cistercian monastery of Sambucina in about 1155; he then moved to the monastery of Corazzo, where in 1177 he was ordained a priest and named abbot. In 1182–83 he was the guest of the abbey of Casamari. After leaving the Cistercians, he lived at first with a companion in the hermitage of Pietralata, then founded the Florense congregation, whose seat was in the monastery of San Giovanni in Fiore, in the mountains of the Sila. His rule represented a more severe version of the Cistercian rule. He died at Canale (Cosenza) on 30th March, 1202. Even if he was never canonized (in fact, as a theologian he was condemned in 1215 by the Lateran Council IV), his relics were venerated by the faithful in the monastery of San Giovanni in Fiore.

His teaching had a great influence on his contemporaries and on the following century. Saint Thomas Aquinas, though condemning certain prophecies, recognizes the saintliness of Joachim's life. Dante places him among the prophets and the luminaries of wisdom, specifically between Saint Thomas and Saint Bonaventura, in Canto XII of the *Paradiso* (139–41):

> . . . e lucemi da lato
> Il calavrese abate Gioacchino
> Di spirito profetico dotato.
>
> (. . . and there shineth at my side
> The Calabrian abbot Joachim
> Endowed with the prophetic spirit.)

His theories influenced the thinking of Saint Bonaventura and of Saint Bernardino of Siena, as also, according to modern scholars, the philosophy of Vico, Mazzini, and even Ibsen. To be sure, Joachim of Fiore exercised a determinant influence on

the various strict religious movements of the 13th century:
the Flagellants, the Spirituals, the Little Friars, and the
Celestines. On the other hand, the Florense order which he
created never spread far and in the 16th century was merged
with the Cistercians.

His fundamental works are the *Concordia Veteris et Novi
Testamenti*, the *Expositio in Apocalipsim*, the *Tractatus super
quatuor Evangelia* and the *Psalterium decem cordarum*.

In Joachim's exegesis the allegorical interpretation of Holy
Scripture is fundamental. In history there exists, he believes,
a "vivens ordo" through which events take place in parallel
cycles, and by observing them it is possible to understand the
significance of present events and sense their further development. Since human history, for Joachim, is summed up in
Christian revelation, which, however, has not yet been fully
achieved, he interprets the Old and the New Testaments not as
closed historical realities, but as symbols through which one
can understand future reality.

For Joachim, a mystery exists, as in the Trinity, in the process
of human history according to a sequence of three periods, of
which the second proceeds from the first, and the third proceeds
from both. In the first period, which began with Moses, it was
the Father who manifested His glory; in the second, it was the
Son; in the third, with the return of Elijah, the Spirit will
dominate. From this eschatological vision Joachim traced the
pattern of the religious reality which was about to be revealed.
In it the Church will not be able to maintain her clerical
structures. The Church of the hierarchy and of symbols will be
succeeded by the community of believers, based on charity,
contemplation, liberty, peace; these are the distinguishing
features of the Kingdom announced by Joachim as imminent.

It would be a mistake to try to place his work in the history of
philosophy or even of theology. "The distinctly predominant
concern in Joachim's writings is never theological; his is a
purely moral and eschatological concern," Buonaiuti has rightly
observed. "Even when he makes war against the theological
systems of his time, all polarized towards a gnostic-logical-

rational interpretation of the mystery of the Trinity, he is never impelled by a determination to set up a system of his own against the others, but rather solely by the more or less conscious need to eliminate the interpretations which might make the dictates of the faith incompatible with the panoramic visions of his philosophy of History . . ." (Ernesto Buonaiuti, *Gioacchino da Fiore—I tempi, la vita, il messaggio*, Rome, 1931, p. 209.)

The Conclave of Perugia

After the death of Pope Nicholas IV, in Rome on 4th April, 1292, the Sacred College of cardinals met in conclave several times in Santa Maria Maggiore, on the Aventine, and in the Minerva, but it had to disband because of an epidemic of the plague.

On 18th October, 1293, the cardinals gathered in Perugia; but time went by without any positive results. The cardinals, reduced to the number of twelve, were in fact divided into two irreconcilable factions, one headed by Cardinal Matteo Rosso Orsini, the other by Cardinal Giacomo Colonna. The cardinals' mood was not made more conciliatory even by the news of revolts and disorders which had broken out in Rome and in other cities of the realm, or by the protests from all sides at the serious inconveniences caused by the lack of a sovereign.

Among the episodes which preceded the conclusion of the long conclave, history has recorded, chiefly in view of what happened later, a heartfelt appeal from Fra Pietro da Morrone to his protector Cardinal Orsini and a direct intervention on the part of Charles II, King of Naples, who came into the meeting hall of the cardinals, which should have remained inaccessible to outsiders (this intervention aroused the remonstrances of Cardinal Benedetto Caetani). When, on 5th July, 1294, after twenty-seven months of waiting, the conclave unanimously elected Fra Pietro da Morrone the new pontiff, the College was reduced to nine cardinals. It was the cardinals themselves who spoke of their complete agreement, for want of another explanation, as a miracle.

Fra Pietro Angelerio

(Celestine V, Pier Celestine)

The essential sources of his biography are to be found in a presumed autobiography, which scholars have refused to authenticate completely, though they have found it rich in convincing details about his adolescence and young manhood. There is also a life of Pietro written by his contemporary and companion in religious life, Fra Bartolomeo da Trasacco, and there is an analogous text, the work of Fra Tommaso da Sulmona. He figures also in the *Opus metricum* of Cardinal Jacopo Stefaneschi, and in the Acts of the cause of his canonization.

He was born at Isernia in 1215 into a family of peasants, the next to last of twelve children. At the age of six, he lost his father. While still very young he became a Benedictine monk in the abbey of Faìfoli in Molise, where he remained three years. His intellectual formation, which remained rather rudimentary, dates from that period. He learned the Latin of the liturgy and the sacred writings, but he didn't form even a vague notion of the profane disciplines, of civil law and history; it was therefore impossible for him to be aware of the crisis of his time, caused by the break-up of the old feudal world and *Christianitas* and the rise of new social needs.

After a brief stay in Rome, where he was ordained a priest, he chose to withdraw to a hermitage. For five years he lived in a cave on the slopes of Mount Morrone, a spur of the Maiella, above Sulmona. Later he sought refuge farther from the inhabited areas, to escape his mounting popularity. Stefaneschi describes him as "tall of stature, robust of body, merry and lively in appearance, sweet and appealing in his speech".

Towards 1240 Fra Pietro interrupted his hermit's life for a while and began to organize in communitarian groups the numerous faithful who were drawn to him by the growing fame of his virtues and his wonders. His congregation received first a *de facto* recognition in 1263 from Pope Urban IV. Later, when the spreading of new religious orders was checked by the revival of a resolution of the Lateran Council of 1215 which forbade them, Fra Pietro journeyed in the spring of 1275 to Lyons, where a new council had met, to beg Gregory X to make an exception in his favour. The pope granted this, on condition, however, that the congregation declare itself simply a branch of the Benedictine order, like the Cluniacensians, Camaldolese, Cistercians, Vallambrosians, Olivetans, Trappists. So its rule followed the Benedictine, differing from it only in a greater severity of penances.

In that first period the new congregation was called simply "the monks of Pietro da Morrone", or else the "Morronese monks", or also "of the abbey of the Holy Spirit at Sulmona". The head of the congregation was the abbot of the Holy Spirit monastery, who was elected by the whole chapter for a three-year period. The monks wore a white habit with a black hood and black mantle. The congregation's coat-of-arms was a cross with an S wound around the lower part of the vertical pole.

In 1294, after the papal coronation of Fra Pietro, who chose for himself the name of Celestine V, the monks of his congregation were also called Celestines. In all that story, both in the deliberation of the conclave and in the first acts of the new pope (the choice of l'Aquila for the coronation, of Naples as temporary apostolic seat, the nomination of new cardinals and the prelates of the Curia) there was an evident, dominant influence of Charles II. It was also evident that the new pope welcomed that protection, though he didn't realize the political consequences that would follow it, for at the same time, with unquestioned sincerity, he lost no opportunity to reaffirm his faith in the Joachimite prophecies and to favour the proselytizing of the Spiritual Franciscans. For that matter, the continuity of the papal policy towards secular States, of which he was only slightly informed, but which he could not easily deny, demanded a political dexterity which he lacked completely. Those personal, insuperable contradictions, more than his lack of intellectual preparation (for uncultured sovereigns have always existed), made his pontificate precarious. The formula of abdication, attributed to Cardinal Benedetto Caetani (Boniface VIII), obviously could not mention them.

The pontificate's brief duration considerably disturbed the life of the Celestine congregation in Italy, but favoured its expansion in France, thanks to the protection of Philip the Fair, who hated Pope Boniface. Celestine convents rose then also in Bohemia, England, Spain, and Belgium. They lived on for several centuries, without any special distinction; in the 17th century their decline became more marked. The revolution of 1789 brought about their suppression in France; Napoleon suppressed them in Italy in 1810.

Entirely ephemeral was the life of the "Poor hermits of Pope Celestine", which absorbed the Spiritual Franciscans just after Celestine V's coronation (September, 1294), giving them a legal position and allowing them to escape the persecution of the Conventual Friars Minor and the ecclesiastical courts. Their peace lasted as long as the pontificate, just over three months. Once Celestine abandoned the tiara, the Spiritual friars were the object of persecutions even more merciless than before. Boniface VIII formally dissolved their makeshift congregation in 1302.

Pier Celestine was captured on 16th May 1295, at Vieste (Gargano), after an unsuccessful attempt to flee to Greece, and he was taken by Guillaume l'Estandard, Constable of the Realm, first to Capua and from there to Anagni, to the residence of Boniface VIII, his successor. After a short time, when Boniface saw it was impossible to achieve any collaboration or agreement, he had Pier Celestine shut up in the nearby fortress of Fumone, above Ferentino, guarded by six knights and thirty men-at-arms. Pier Celestine died there on 19th May, 1296, at the age of eighty-one.

A rumour immediately spread that he had been assassinated by order of Boniface. The evidence for and against this serious accusation has been discussed a great deal, though no certain conclusion has ever been reached. Boniface's adversaries mentioned, among other things, the discovery of a chisel which was the presumed murder weapon. Greater significance may be attached to certain early iconographic depictions. The image of San Pier Celestine, with the martyr's palm, appears in relief on the main bell of the abbey of the Holy Spirit at Sulmona; he is also so depicted in the *Digestum Scripturarum Coelestinianae Congregationis* (Pansa Collection, Sulmona, Vol. II, p. 80) and in a fresco by an Abruzzese painter of the 14th century in the hermitage of Sant'Onofrio. It is also indicative that, in our own time, the German Catholic dramatist Reinhold Schneider has fully accepted the story of the assassination in his Celestinian play (*Der grosse Verzicht*, Insel Verlag, 1950, Act V, scene ii).

Pier Celestine was proclaimed a saint on 5th May, 1313, by Pope Clement V in Avignon.

But the act of his canonization was also shrouded in ambiguity, since it was hastened not only by the fame of his virtues and his miracles, but also by the determined intervention of Philip the Fair, out of hatred for the memory of Boniface VIII.

Of the various monks who appear in the play, Fra Bartolomeo da Trasacco, Fra Angelo da Caramanico and Fra Tommaso da Sulmona are historical figures.

As to the canon *Romanum Pontificem posse libere resignare* adopted by Celestine V before his abdication and included by Boniface VIII in the body of canon law, it is still held valid by the most authoritative legal experts of the Church. After Celestine V, Gregory XII also made use of it.

Pietro da Fossombrone

(*Angelo Clareno*)

He was born at Chiarino, near Recanati (according to others, at Fossombrone, also in the vicinity), and, as a young man, he joined the Franciscan movement. Soon he too was involved in the serious disagreement which divided the movement and which, one might say, was congenital in it. In fact, while Saint Francis was still living, two opposing bodies of opinion had already taken shape, on the question of how to understand and apply the rule, especially in its fundamental aspect of poverty. The majority (*fratres de communitate*) asked for freer dispensations which would permit the opening of large convents in the cities and the access to chairs of study; whereas the minority (*fratres spirituales*) fought for a strict, literal observance of the rule, which in their deference they considered almost equal to the Gospels. The ascetic severity of these Spiritual friars was accompanied by an open eschatological anxiety. During the 13th century other groups, more or less strict, broke away at least verbally from the Franciscan order; and they were generally called Little Friars or Devotees or Zealots or similar denominations, but, as far as discipline and morality are concerned, they were often quite different from the Spiritual friars. The inquisitorial authorities frequently and purposely confused one with the other in order to discredit the opposition as a whole.

Pietro da Fossombrone followed the lead of Pietro Olivi and Umbertino da Casale, and with Pietro da Macerata and Jacopone da Todi and others, he was among the outstanding animators of the movement of the Spiritual friars, which had no central organization but was directed locally by those persons who, through gifts of character or mind, emerged as leaders. Pietro da Fossombrone headed the movement in the Marches and, thanks to their geographical vicinity, soon came into contact with the Morronese monks and established bonds of solidarity with Fra Pietro Angelerio. With the formation of the congregation of the "Pauperes heremite Domini Celestini", Pietro da Fossombrone took the name of Angelo Clareno, and it is under this name that he was remembered by posterity.

What information we have about him describes him as a truly superior man, admired even by his adversaries for the saintliness of his life and his teaching. Nevertheless, his life was harassed, hard, and stormy. (See: Arsenio Frugoni, in *Celestiniana*, the chapter "Dai *Pauperes heremite Domini Celestini* ai *Fraticelli de Paupere vita*", Rome, 1954, pp. 125–67.) Briefly, we may recall that he was imprisoned a first time in 1276 and condemned by the ecclesiastic court to prison for life. This punishment, in certain cases, was aggravated by privation of the sacraments and prohibition of all reading. Released in 1289, he was sent to Cilicia (in southern Armenia), where a pious sovereign, Haiton, granted religious exiles the right of asylum. Still, the Spiritual friars were the victims of plots and aggression on the part of the Conventual Franciscans. Pietro had secretly returned to Italy and was living a clandestine life when, in the summer of 1294, Fra Pietro Angelerio was elected pope.

The *modus vivendi* whereby the Spiritual friars could profit by the new pope's protection without renouncing their essential principles did not last long. Celestine's abdication was followed by an immediate and harsher persecution from Boniface VIII and a new diaspora. With a group of his followers Clareno took refuge at Achaia and, from there, in 1298, in Thessalia. He came back to Italy again in 1305 and for several years lived in hiding in the vicinity of Rome, trying to reconstruct the movement of the Spiritual friars. In 1311 he moved to Avignon, where he remained until 1318. The preceding year he was excommunicated by the Bull "Sancta Romana Ecclesia", which also formally dissolved the congregation of the Poor Hermits (13th December, 1317). Returning to Italy, he resumed his clandestine activity, first near Subiaco, then in Lucania, where he died on 15th June, 1337.

On the sad history of the Spiritual friars Clareno himself has left us a vehement pamphlet entitled *Historia septem tribulationum Ordinis Minorum.* The first of these seven tribulations recalls how when Saint Francis had left for the East, Fra Elia forced a false and opportunistic orientation on the Order; the second narrates what happened immediately after the death of Saint Francis; the third, the period of Crescenzio di Ancona; the fourth, the period of Saint Bonaventura; the fifth, the persecution of Giovanni Olivi; the sixth, the abdication of Celestine V. The seventh was never written.

What does such a singular experience represent in the general religious crisis of that period? It might be useful to quote the opinion of a historian:

"The sects all have certain beliefs which are more properly religious and moral: a Church that must be in the community of the faithful; the ability of any Christian to administer the sacraments and preach the word of Christ; restoration of apostolic life in its entirety. But then, some more, some less, they want the Church and the clergy to be poor as in the times before Constantine and Sylvester; they make manual labour obligatory for the pastors of the community; they condemn inequality among men; they have vague theoretical tones, and even some practices, of communism; they do not understand or want to understand prayers and sacred books in Latin; they hark back to the Gospels to deny all earthly power and any legitimacy of bodily punishment, any tribute to the state or tithe to the Church. Who are these heretics then? They are smiths, tailors, weavers, carders, peasants; 'illiterate and idiot' people, as their adversaries call them and as they too, at times, like to call themselves; ignorant, that is, and contemptuous of that culture of the Church and the upper classes to which the humble people felt alien. . . ." (Gioacchino Volpe, *Movimenti religiosi e sette ereticali nellà società medievale italiana, Secoli XI–XIV*, Florence, 1961, p. 247.)

Jacopone da Todi

A member of the noble Benedetti family of Todi, Jacopone was born on an unknown date around 1240. There is little precise information about his life, but he was certainly a man of culture and wealth. In his poetry, there are echoes of the Sicilian lyric as well as French and Provençal turns of phrase. About 1268 he was converted to a severe ascetic life, and for about ten years he was a wandering mendicant. In 1278 he entered the order of the Friars Minor, where he joined with the supporters of the strict rule and made common cause with the Spiritual friars. His spirit was not bowed by persecutions. His *Lauds* clearly drew on the Franciscan tradition; rather than the lyrical expression of personal feelings, they were texts meant to edify, a complement to preaching. He fought the ambition and vainglory which are born from an excessive desire of learning (invective against Paris) and he exalted humility, the most Franciscan of virtues.

His poetic gift and his sectarian passion did not, however, blind him to the difficulties of the period. Therefore, when Celestine was elected pope in July, 1294, Jacopone did not share the illusions of his own Spiritual Franciscan brothers and addressed to the pope the famous admonition that began:

> Che farai Pier da Morrone?
> Se' venuto al paragone . . .
>
> (What will you do, Pier da Morrone?
> You to the fray now have come.)

Which was followed, in clear terms, by the explanation of the poet's mistrust:

> The order of Cardinals
> has sunk to low estate;
> each has the intention
> of enriching his family.

Be on guard against those with prebends,
you will always find them hungry;
their thirst is so great
that no potion slakes it.

Be on guard against the barrators
who make white seem black;
if you cannot defend yourself well
you will sing a sorrowful song.

Since he had foreseen it, Jacopone was not cast down when the failure of Celestine's pontificate was evident, and he continued his fight even after Boniface VIII had dissolved the movement of the Spiritual friars. In some vehement Lauds he called Boniface the "new anti-Christ". According to Salvatorelli (*L'Italia comunale dal secolo XI alla metà del secolo XIV*, Milan, 1940, p. 707), Jacopone founded, with some other Spiritual friars, a hermitage near Palestrina similar to that of the *pauperes heremite* in the Abruzzi.

Jacopone allowed himself to become involved in the Colonnas' armed plot against Boniface, he signed the manifesto of Lunghezza (10th May, 1297), which declared the pope deposed. For this the writer was excommunicated. When Palestrina, the Colonna citadel, was taken, Jacopone was found there, was tried, and imprisoned in a convent. He was freed and his excommunication annulled only after Boniface's death. He spent his last years in the convent of the Poor Clares at San Lorenzo di Collazzone, between Perugia and Todi, where he died on Christmas day, 1306.

Boniface VIII

(*Benedetto Caetani*)

Boniface VIII was the real antagonist of Pier Celestine and of the religious movements which took a strict view of the Christian's duties and the function of the Church in public life.

He was born in Anagni in 1235, and after serious study of law in Todi and Bologna he was sent on various confidential missions by the Holy See to the court of Saint Louis and to London. His career in the Curia was rapid and not only because of the influence of his family. He was considered wise, ambitious, haughty; and, like other officials, corruptible and a corruptor. In the long Perugia conclave, since his time had not yet come, he remained a discreet spectator of the exhausting conflict between the Orsinis and the Colonnas; but he distinguished himself with his protest against the intervention of Charles II in a meeting that was supposed to be inaccessible for outsiders.

During Celestine V's pontificate, realizing its precariousness, he worked skilfully for his own succession. There are grotesque legends about the expedients he adopted to hasten the end: in writing this play we have not taken them into any account. The conclave which met in the Castelnuovo in Naples on 23rd December 1294 (after ten days of *sede vacante*, according to the Gregorian rules re-established by Celestine), lasted barely two days: Cardinal Caetani was elected on the third ballot.

Boniface VIII's pontificate remains a crucial point in the history of relations between the Church and the States. If its final outcome was humiliating for him and for the Church, this was not because of any personal weakness or inability of his, but because of the anachronism of the vision by which he had allowed himself to be led. His concept, coherently expressed in a great number of decrees and bulls which culminated in the "Unam Sanctam" of 1303, extended the sphere of ecclesiastic power until it absorbed and dominated the temporal power of

princes: papal power knew practically no limits, it was "pleni-
tudo potestatis", since it was of divine origin. It was a purely
mediaeval concept, carried to its extreme logical consequences,
proclaimed, however, in a period when the Middle Ages were
coming to an end and the great nations were already emerging.

In the new situation papal anathemas had lost their old
efficacy. The sovereignty of Philip the Fair was not in the least
affected by Boniface's maledictions, and since the king was
supported by the French clergy, as well as by the nobility and
the bourgeoisie, he was even able to take the counter-offensive.
At the Louvre Council, Guillaume de Plessis presented a
resolution with twenty-nine articles against Boniface, containing
accusations of heresy, immorality, and superstition. Guillaume
de Nogaret, Philip's adviser, was bold enough to conceive a
reversal of relations with Rome, which would have made France
the first daughter of the Church and would have transferred the
papal seat to Avignon. The same Nogaret, with Sciarra Colonna,
was the sad hero of the aggression against Boniface in his
residence in Anagni, which outraged even many adversaries of
the pope's policy. Dante was among those who considered the
offence as if it had been directed against Christ himself:

> Veggio in Alagna intrar lo fiordaliso
> e nel vicario suo Cristo esser catto.
> Veggiolo un'altra volta esser deriso;
> veggio rinovellar l'aceto e 'l fele . . .
>
> (*Purgatorio* XX, 86–90)
>
> (I see the fleur-de-lys enter Alagna, and in his
> vicar, Christ made captive. I see him mocked again,
> I see the vinegar and gall renewed . . .)

This attack took place on 7th September, 1303; on the 12th of
the following month Boniface died. He was condemned by his
successor Clement V, was tried in the ecumenical Council of
Vienne and his political Bulls were annulled.

Dante and Celestine

The majority of Dante's commentators, from the very first (Jacopo della Lana, Pietro di Dante, Boccaccio) have identified, though with some reservations, Celestine V as the character indicated in the third Canto of the Inferno, the man who "*fece per viltà il gran rifiuto*" (out of cowardice made the great refusal). The *gran rifiuto* would thus refer to the refusal of the pontificate, which Celestine decided upon, considering himself unsuited to bearing the weight of the government of the Church.

The accusation of "cowardice" (which has caused others, for example Scartazzini and Pietrobono, to doubt it could mean Celestine V) has been explained with the argument that, in consequence of that abdication, Boniface VIII was elected pope. And Dante hated Boniface for his theocratic ideas and as fomenter of the movement which established the government of the Blacks in Florence and drove the poet into exile. According to the opinion of a majority of scholars, the violence of the invective could be directed only against a contemporary, known to Dante, if not in person then through events whose consequences he had felt personally.

This opinion is shared, among modern commentators, by Steiner, Rossi, and Sapegno. The last of these has, however, added: "The identification remains highly uncertain, and it has persisted only because almost all the other suggestions made by one scholar or another are even less convincing."

Among other names proposed, first of all, there is that of Esau, who ceded his birthright to his brother Jacob. This was the thesis of Benvenuto Rambaldi da Imola, who nevertheless reports that, even in his day, the most accredited opinion was that the figure was Celestine V. Other suggestions have been Pilate, Diocletian, Julian the Apostate, Romulus Augustulus, and among Dante's contemporaries, Giano della Bella and Vieri de' Cerchi.

Petrarch and Celestine

The treatise *De vita solitaria* of Petrarch contains an impassioned apologetic of Pier Celestine, from which we quote the following excerpts:

". . . This gesture (the abdication) of the solitary and Holy Father (Celestine) may be attributed by those who will to cowardice of spirit, since the diversity of temperaments allows us to express on the same argument opinions which are not only different, but conflicting. For myself, I believe the gesture was above all useful to himself and to the world.

"For both, in fact, that lofty dignity could be full of dangers, and risks, and disturbances, because of Pietro's inexperience of human things—he had neglected them in order to contemplate divine things too much—and because of his constant love of solitude. How Christ received such an act is clear thanks to a miracle which God worked, through him, the day after his renunciation: a miracle which surely would not have taken place if God had disapproved of what Celestine had done. I consider his act as the act of a most lofty and free spirit which knew no impositions, of a truly divine spirit; and I think a man could not have so acted if he had not rightly evaluated human affairs, and had not set beneath his foot the proud head of fortune . . .

"The joy and the enthusiasm of his descent bear witness to how sad his ascent had been and how contrary to his aspirations. From persons who saw him I have heard it said that he escaped with immense joy, his eyes and his countenance bearing the signs of his spiritual happiness, when, free at last and restored to himself, he went away from the council not as if he had relieved his back of a moderate burden but as if he had freed his neck of a terrible axe, thus there shone in his countenance I know not what angelic light. And rightly: he well knew, in fact, what he was to find, and he was not unaware of what he was leaving. From toil he was returning to repose, from vain arguments to divine conversation, he was abandoning the city, he was going with his spirit—and if his successor's craftiness had not opposed it—with his body, to a steep and difficult mountain, I agree; but beyond it there would open to him an easy path to celestial things. Oh, if only I had lived with him! Among so many solitaries, with him alone I would especially have liked to live, because on no other occasion has my desire been closer to the thing desired. The interval that separates us is not great, if he had only delayed, or I had hastened a little, we would have trod together the path of this life, which he followed with our fathers. And in such a brief space of time, how many were the convents of the sacred order that he founded all through Italy, even to the Alps! And already, I hear it said, this devotion, spreading, has crossed the Alps. . . ."

(Francesco Petrarca, *De vita solitaria*, Book Two, edited by Guido Martellotti, in the volume of Petrarch's *Prose*, published by Riccardo Ricciardi, Milan-Naples, 1955, pp. 475–481.)

About the Author

Ignazio Silone was born in Pescina dei Marsik, a village in the Abruzzi Apennines, in 1900. His father was a small landowner, his mother a weaver. He received his early schooling in Pescina and then studied for the priesthood in Catholic institutions in various Italian towns.

During World War I, at the age of seventeen, he was appointed secretary of the land workers for the Abruzzi district. He became deeply involved in the antiwar movement, and after Mussolini's takeover, in the Communist underground, fighting the Fascist regime. In 1930, after having been imprisoned in and expelled from several European countries, he settled in Switzerland, where, in 1940, he organized a network of Socialist underground resistance groups against the Fascists. He returned to Italy in 1944. Since 1950, he has not been associated with any political group.

Mr. Silone is the author of *The Story of a Humble Christian, Emergency Exit, Bread and Wine, The Fox and the Camelias, Fontamara, The Secret of Luca, A Handful of Blackberries, And He Hid Himself, The Seed Beneath the Snow, The School for Dictators,* and *Mr. Aristotle.*